800 Days on the Eastern Front

800 Days on the Eastern Front

A Russian Soldier Remembers World War II

Nikolai Litvin
Translated and Edited by Stuart Britton

University Press of Kansas

Published by the University Press of Kansas (Lawrence, Kansas 66049), which
was organized by the Kansas Board of Regents and is operated and funded by
Emporia State University, Fort Hays State University, Kansas State University,
Pittsburg State University, the University of Kansas, and Wichita State University

ISBN 978-0-7006-1517-9

Printed in the United States of America

To the Soldier of Victory

Contents

Contents

Illustrations

Maps

Photographs

Editor's Note

In 2004, I began a small project to gather oral histories from Russian veterans of what they call the Great Patriotic War—the Eastern Front of World War II. I had seen an increasing number of memoirs from American veterans of World War II, and also from German veterans of that war. I was aware that this generation, who had lived through this titanic global struggle, was slipping away, and the days when we can listen to their voices are numbered. But I was also aware that the Russian voice was largely missing from the new stream of memoirs. I was determined in some small way to gather the experiences and stories of the average Russian soldier, so that they may become better known in the West.

The commanding officers have had their time to speak and publish. Like most students of the war, I grew up on the personal stories and reminiscences of the great captains of the war: men like Bradley, Guderian, von Manstein, and Zhukov. And while, to varying degrees, these commanders expressed understanding of or sympathy for the hardships of the frontline soldier, they primarily operated on a level totally remote to the man huddled and shivering in the trenches. Their principal concerns were not with where they would get their next meal, or with the lice infesting their uniforms. Rather, they were with feeding and equipping masses of soldiers, and with moving them efficiently from point A to point B, and with how best to engage the enemy. They had political concerns and rivalries with other commanders and participated in planning sessions at the highest levels. Later, I had the opportunity to read the memoirs of divisional commanders and battalion commanders. These men were closer to the front lines and had more frequent interaction with the privates and sergeants who served in the front lines.

I understood that the surviving voices today had been young men and women in 1941, and that their experience of the war was that of the average soldier: the private, the gun team commander, the medic, or the tank driver. Gradually, we are learning more about the perspective and experiences of the frontline soldier, especially the American, British, and German soldier. But the primary struggle in the European theater of operations was not between the Western

Allies and Germany. It was between Germany and the Soviet Union. Some of the recent memoirs are from German soldiers who served in this colossal struggle against the Soviet Union. Up until this point, however, we have heard relatively little from the average Russian soldier. In some small way, I hope with this project to redress this imbalance.

To begin the interview project, I contacted Svetlana Nizhevskaia of Krasnodar, Russia. She quickly agreed to locate Russian veterans who might be willing to speak to me about their wartime experiences. Once Svetlana obtained the agreement of a veteran to participate, I would send her lists of questions, and she would use these to conduct the interview. She taped each interview and then transcribed the tapes into Russian texts that she would e-mail back to me. It was a cumbersome, laborious process, but we quickly began to obtain some interesting material.

The second veteran Svetlana interviewed was Nikolai Litvin. During the course of their first interview, Litvin casually mentioned that he had written a memoir back in 1962, during the brief "thaw" in Soviet arts and literature initiated by Khrushchev. Before Litvin could finish the memoir and find a publisher, however, Khrushchev was deposed, and the Brezhnev leadership reasserted tight controls over Soviet publishing. Thus, Litvin's memoir had lain unpublished in his desk for more than forty years. He asked Svetlana if I would be interested in editing his memoir for publication in the West.

Naturally, I jumped at the opportunity. One of the problems with interviewing these elderly veterans about their wartime experiences is simply that they have forgotten many details of the war, and their memory plays tricks with other facts. This problem is compounded in the Soviet experience by the fact that soldiers in the Red Army were not allowed to keep diaries, and letters home were tightly censored. Often they could say little more than "I am fine. If I die, please consider me a Communist." So the Russian veterans had no contemporary personal, written record to which they could refer.

Because Litvin penned his memoir in 1962, his memory was much fresher at the time of writing than it could be today, and he could recall many more names and details. Moreover, since the war, Litvin has been active in veterans' circles, and to the extent that he could, he researched and studied the battles and campaigns in which he was involved.

Svetlana Nizhevskaia sent me the memoir, and I began translating it into English. I often had questions about incidents in the memoir, and I frequently e-mailed additional questions for Litvin to Svetlana. She would then interview Litvin again and e-mail me his responses. Nikolai demonstrated enormous patience with my many questions, never failing to give me an honest, clear answer—even on very delicate topics. At times, he sent me material from his personal library.

The original memoir was written in a simple, straightforward style—little more than a chronological narrative of events. It was remarkably free of Soviet-era propaganda, which colored and distorted many officers' memoirs published during the Soviet years. But it also lacked much detail. During the war, Litvin naturally knew little about the "larger picture," the battle and campaign plans. From day to day, he rarely knew where he was going, and rarely understood why. In addition, Litvin is a modest man, and like many Russian veterans, he was reluctant to speak in personal terms. Once I wrote to him, "Nikolai, you always use the term 'We.' It makes it difficult for me to identify the actor—was it your immediate circle of comrades, your battery, your battalion, your division, or your army? Please, I want to see the word 'I' more often in your memoir." He replied in characteristically modest style, "Stuart, I cannot use the word 'I.' I accomplished nothing in the war by myself, and what I did mattered little. It was only the effort of millions of my comrades that accomplished anything and brought us victory."

In its bare outlines, however, I could tell that Litvin's memoir had the potential to become a highly interesting document. He was trained as an airborne soldier but never made a combat jump. At various times during the war, he served as an antitank gunner, a heavy machine gunner, a driver, and a chauffeur. Due to a poor decision to leave his post in response to a written request, rather than an order, he was arrested and sentenced to serve in a penal battalion. Such a sentence was often a death sentence, as these penal battalions were called upon to lead any assault upon enemy fortifications. During the course of the war, he was wounded three times, testifying to his active service. Yet he could also offer eyewitness observations of generals and their staff operations. So I began a lengthy, sometimes intensive period of interviews with him.

Gradually, Litvin grew comfortable with me and began to share more personal stories and memories. With his permission, I incorporated these stories into appropriate places in the memoir, and his interview answers did much to add accuracy, color, and drama to the memoir. In addition, Litvin has become a student of the war; he often provided me with other published Russian materials and information about his campaigns and battles. He also sent me photographs from his personal collection for the memoir.

In addition to translating his memoir and interviewing Litvin for additional material and detail, I thought it beneficial to add contextual commentary at various points in the memoir so the reader will understand how Litvin's personal narrative fits into the higher level of Soviet planning and the Red Army's operations during the war. I have italicized my commentary throughout this book, in order to distinguish it from Litvin's narrative. At other times, I tucked bits of historical information into footnotes, to explain potentially unfamiliar Russian terms, offer further description of the weapons he mentions, or offer further insight into what happened. I hope the reader will find this additional material informative, and not too intrusive.

Like Litvin, I am very reluctant to use the word "I" with respect to this memoir. The memoir is Litvin's, of course, and without his willingness to share it with me, I would have had no opportunity to collaborate on this book. It was a genuine pleasure and privilege to work with Litvin, even if we have not yet met in person. I highly admire his sincerity, patience, and willingness to share his experiences with the Western reader.

This book also depended upon the invaluable assistance of Svetlana Nizhevskaia. Her unflagging dedication to the interview process and her willingness to spend long hours transcribing the tapes for me were absolutely critical to the book. She also offered reassurance whenever I doubted a piece of my translation, and at other times helped with some unfamiliar Russian phrase or expression. Her sensitive nature and courteous personality undoubtedly helped relax Litvin during the interviews, and she offered constant support and encouragement to me whenever I faltered or grew discouraged. I hope that our collaboration continues to bear fruit in the future.

Colonel David M. Glantz (U.S. Army, retired) was another invaluable source of assistance on the book. He readily and unfailingly responded to my questions about campaign specifics or Red Army units and orders of battle, offered timely sage advice, and kindly agreed to read a draft of the memoir. His own sterling record of meticulous research into Soviet archival records and documents, and his numerous publications on the Eastern Front, constantly served as sources of information and inspiration.

I also want to thank Dr. Roger Reese, Professor of History at Texas A&M University, for his careful reading of the manuscript. His keen eye for detail uncovered several problems with translation and transliteration of the Russian language in the draft of the manuscript and also helped strengthen the final draft in several ways.

I offer a tip of my cap to Dr. Charles Dannehl, my former graduate school colleague and now Professor of Political Science at Bradley University. His knowledge of automobile mechanics helped me through a particularly knotty piece of translation.

Of course, any errors of fact or translation in this book are strictly my responsibility alone. I hope the reader will not let any such mistakes diminish Litvin's straightforward memoir, his sincere answers to my questions, and his duty to his country during a most terrible war.

I also want to extend my deep appreciation to Michael Briggs, Editor in Chief of the University Press of Kansas. He was a constant source of support and prompt answers to my questions as I prepared the final manuscript.

Finally, I owe a sincere debt to my wife, Shana, who selflessly kept the house afloat financially while I pursued this venture. It has indeed been a long and winding road.

Chapter 1

I Become an Airborne Soldier

I was born on 20 June 1923 in the village of Grigorevka, forty kilometers south of the city of Petropavlovsk in western Siberia. My parents were peasants, and I was one of four sons born to them. After the end of the Russian Civil War, my father worked as a tractor mechanic.

In 1927, my grandfather and my uncles formed an agricultural cooperative. They farmed an area of approximately five square kilometers. Through government loans, they acquired a tractor, a threshing machine, a grain harvesting machine, and other farm machinery and inventory. In its first year of operation, the co-op grew a very tall crop of wheat, which was sufficient to pay off the government loan.

At the end of 1929, our family moved to Nikolaev in the Ukraine, where my father worked at a shipbuilding factory. I began my studies at a school in Nikolaev in 1931. In 1933, the Ukraine began experiencing a terrible famine.[1] In order to save the family from starvation, we moved to Omsk Oblast, where my father worked in a garage as a mechanic for the "Fighting" state farm [*sovkhoz*]. It was here where I completed fourth grade and joined the Young Pioneers,[2] together with my brother. I recall that there was a shortage of ties and neckerchiefs then, and my brother and I once wrote a letter to Stalin: "Comrade Stalin, please send neckerchiefs to me and my brother." Soon, neckerchiefs reappeared in the shops, but then we received a letter from the district committee: "Children, we hope you now have your neckerchiefs, but in the future, we ask you not to trouble Stalin with such matters."

About this time, my parents sent me back to my birthplace, Grigorevka, to help my grandfather and grandmother on the co-op. I completed the seventh class of my education there. In training there, the local youth selected me to be the chairman of the civil defense organization. By this time, I had earned many badges through the Young Pioneers, including defense badges, the "Voroshilov Rifleman,"[3] sanitation and chemical defense badges, and the "Readiness for Labor and Defense." No one else in the village had so many such honors! I organized training for the youth in shooting and self-defense. Our school took first place in the district competitions. In October 1938, I was accepted into the Komsomol, the Communist Youth League, which was the preparatory stage to Party membership.

In August 1939 I entered the Petropavlovsk Technical School for Geotechnical Engineering. By the spring of 1941, we had finished the academic portion of our training and had begun field training in geodesics. I was eighteen years old.

The Outbreak of War

On the morning of Sunday, 22 June 1941, I woke up, leaned over, and turned on my radio. For some reason I didn't hear the physical exercise program that normally played on the radio at that time of the morning. Instead, the radio was playing military march music continuously. Later that morning, my father dropped by to see me and suggested we go for a beer. It was a warm day. Around noon, the martial music on the radio was interrupted by an official communication. Foreign Minister Molotov was speaking: "Citizens and *kolkhozniki*[4] . . . Fascist Germany has attacked us. . . . " A thought immediately flashed through my mind: "Father will first be called to the front, then my brother Alexander (Shurka), then me. My father and I will return, but Shurka will not." And that is precisely what happened. Shurka was two years younger than me.

The next day, when we went to school, the school administration announced that it was terminating our geodesic training. The male students were immediately to undergo training as tractor operators, the female students as dispatchers for the machine tractor stations that served farms in the area. Why tractor operators? Because when the war began, existing tractor operators were mobilized for the front, while someone still needed to harvest the fields. So they prepared us for the job.

The director of the local machine tractor station was an Order of Lenin recipient. For a month, we trained hard to learn how to operate and repair the tractors and machinery. Then he sent us to a kolkhoz to prepare for the upcoming harvest. When we arrived, we found no tractors waiting for us. We had to repair some broken-down tractors for our own eventual use. Eventually, I was assigned to operate a ChTZ—a tractor from the Cheliabinsk Tractor Factory. We drove around on our tractors for a while, to get the feel of handling our machines, and in the evening the director came and organized us into a tractor brigade.

The harvest began. For some reason, my tractor ran slowly and kept falling behind the other tractors. I was embarrassed, so embarrassed that later that night, I had a dream. In my dream, Engineer Zubkov, who had trained us on the tractors, visited our tractor brigade. I asked him, "Why is my tractor moving so slowly?" And in my dream, he answered, "Hey, you dunderhead, tighten up the governor, and your machine will run faster." I woke up with a start at 2:00 A.M., jumped out of bed, ran to the tractor, tightened the governor—and the next day, my tractor indeed ran faster.

I worked there until the harvest finished on 25 September 1941. When the harvest work ended, we returned to the technical school to begin our third year of study in land surveying and topography. Then suddenly the government passed a decree to shorten our course of study from four years to three.

During our third and now final year of study, we also engaged in civil defense and paramilitary training. I trained in airborne assault techniques, such as parachute jumping and glider landings. Other students studied chemical defense [flame-throwing] measures. In our Komsomol (Communist Youth League) organization we even had a motto: "Each member should earn four badges: the 'Voroshilov Rifleman' (for shooting accuracy), the 'Readiness for Anti-Air Defense,' the 'Readiness for Labor and Defense,' and the 'Readiness for Sanitary Defense.'"

In the fall of 1941, the 52nd Aviation Squadron arrived in our city. They trained civilian pilots, including volunteers from our technical school. Incidentally, when the war started, training at the technical school became no longer free, but I didn't have to pay: education was free for the children of *frontoviki* [frontline soldiers].

I Volunteer for the Airborne

Shortly after my final year of study, they wrote out a certificate for me to leave for graduate practice in Pavlodar. But by that time, I badly wanted to go to the front, even though I had an education waiver until the completion of my technical training. Sometimes I could hear people around me saying, "He's paid them all off! Look at him walking around like such a smart aleck!" Their words shamed me.

So I went to the military enlistment office and began to pester them to take me into the Red Army. The military commissar refused: "When it is necessary, we'll come for you." But at that time, a lieutenant arrived to recruit troops for the airborne forces. I appealed to him. He asked, "Are you a Komsomol member?"

"Yes," I said, "I have made thirty-seven parachute jumps, and I'm a third category fencer. I have glider and ski experience."

The lieutenant warned me that airborne troops were already 90 percent dead men walking but told me that if I persisted, he would accept me—only on the condition that the oblast Komsomol committee would give me a recommendation.

I ran to the oblast Komsomol committee and found an acquaintance of mine, Genka Uporov, sitting there. He also was a former student of the technical school but had left to fight in the "Winter War" against Finland and had returned crippled, with the Order of the Red Banner. He tried to persuade me not to enter the airborne forces but gave me a recommendation nonetheless.

On 20 September 1942, I was brought to Liubertsy, near Moscow, to the 1st Airborne Corps. Ten such corps were forming up there, by order of Stalin. [*Here Litvin could not resist a little joke.*] He wanted to use them to subjugate all of Europe, and fling them upon all the capitals of Europe. Hitler simply outpaced him, and was already in France, Austria, and Czechoslovakia. The Americans conquered half the world with the help of the 82nd Airborne!

I found approximately forty volunteers from my city in Liubertsy. The command supplemented us with men who had been imprisoned for minor violations: Twenty minutes late—straight to jail. They gathered an entire echelon in this fashion.

In Liubertsy, they took us first to a bathhouse and then distributed the uniforms. The commissar of the echelon, Tumarbekov, was ordered to select 100 men for a special unit—a separate mortar battalion [*divizion*] attached to corps' headquarters. My assignment was with this mortar battalion.

At that point we had no artillery, and we carried everything ourselves, even our mortars. We each carried a PPSh submachine gun, a Finnish knife, two grenades (one antitank, one antipersonnel), 500 rounds of ammunition, a sapper's shovel, a water bottle, and a meal kit. Some of us carried the barrels of the mortars; others carried the bases or the mortar shells.

The Northwestern Front: Demiansk and Staraia Rusa

In the winter of 1942, German Army Group North's 16th Army held a narrow salient deep into the Soviet lines at Demiansk. The Soviet Stavka had marked this salient for elimination but held even more ambitious goals for the offensive in this sector. The Stavka hoped that the simultaneous blows of Northwestern Front's 1st Shock Army and 27th Army on opposite sides of the Demiansk corridor would crush the corridor leading into the Demiansk pocket and simultaneously tear open a gap in the German defenses. This would allow the 1st Tank Army to crash through into the German rear toward Stoltsy and Luga, thereby unhinging Army Group North's Sixteenth Army from its northern neighbor, the Eighteenth Army encircling Leningrad.

Litvin's 4th Guards Airborne Division, along with other airborne divisions formed in the "second wave" of Stalin's attempt to create an airborne force, was sent to Northwestern Front's 1st Shock Army to support its offensive against the southern side of the Demiansk corridor. Although all but one regiment of his division remained in reserve, Litvin's narrative is noteworthy for the difficulties he details under which the Soviet infantry labored at this point in the war on this sector of the front. Hunger was a real problem, even for such an elite infantry formation, while they labored under difficult late winter conditions in boggy terrain with insufficient transportation.

In December 1942, our airborne corps was reorganized into the 4th Guards Airborne Division.[5] They took the mortars from us and gave us instead 45-mm antitank guns and parachutes for them. On 3 February 1943 came the order for our departure to the front, to join the Northwestern Front's 1st Shock Army south of Lake Il'men. We turned in our parachutes and received our combat loads. We spent the first night in Khimki and then moved by rail to Klina. Our battery reached the home of Tchaikovsky, the famous composer, and discovered that the Germans had been using it as a stable for their horses. We built campfires and spent the night there. The next day we passed through Torzhok and reached Ostashkov, south of Lake Il'men. When we arrived, we received a hot meal and skis. We waited here from 13 February until 15 February while the entire division was concentrating. On 15 February, the division moved out on skis toward our staging point for the coming offensive—a point about twenty kilometers southwest of Staraia Rusa, and east of Kholm.

There were thousands of vehicles in the area! Once, one truck created a traffic jam along the way. Traffic jams were dangerous—we had no air cover, and we were moving in a dangerously dense formation: eight divisions, 120,000 people. The order came immediately: "Shoot the driver!" Near Astratovo we stopped in a forest. The terrain in the area was very swampy. There was a light frost, and it was around twenty degrees Fahrenheit.

Here our division joined the 18th Guards Rifle Corps, which was part of the 1st Shock Army of the Northwestern Front. Ever since the first winter offensive of 1941–1942, the 1st Shock Army had been locked in savage fighting with the Germans, trying to liquidate the "Ramushevo corridor" into the Demiansk pocket. It had suffered enormous casualties in repeated attempts to cut the Ramushevo corridor but had not accomplished that objective. In the waning weeks of the 1942 winter offensive, Stalin and the Stavka wanted to make one more effort to cut the corridor and eliminate the Demiansk salient.

Before the offensive, we had to defend the single road that served as the supply route to this sector of the front. There were no food supplies. We found a dead horse and lived off it for two weeks, until food supplies finally arrived. We had a PTR antitank rifle company with us, many of its men fresh out of prison. The company's sergeant major, Tumarbekov, one day suggested, "Let's raid the Fritzes!"

The situation was that on the left bank of the Parusia River, the Germans and Finns had been sitting for one and a half years, sheltered in bunkers and pillboxes.[6] The small river at that time was frozen and covered with snow and frozen corpses. We hatched a plan, then crawled up to the German lines and waited for the moment when the Germans changed garrisons. The order came, "Let's go!" A desultory crossfire erupted and continued for nearly two hours. We held fire from our 45-mm guns, however, as at that time our ammunition supply was quite low—only two rounds per barrel. Somehow our raiding party reached their food stores and managed to return to our lines without losses. In the morning, the commander of the regiment summoned Tumarbekov and gave him a formal reprimand. To all the others, he gave medals!

The Northwestern Front's offensive began on 26 February 1943, in the area of the Ramushevo salient. Our attack had been due to begin 15 February, but it had been badly delayed by difficulties in assembling the attack force due to the lack of roads in the boggy, forested region. For example, the 1st, 2nd, 3rd, and 4th Guards Airborne Divisions arrived on time, but without their artillery, combat supplies, and provisions. Other units, including the ski brigades, arrived at the point of concentration only in the days after 20 February.

The larger objective of the 1st Shock Army was to attack the "neck" of the German Demiansk salient from the south, acting jointly with the 27th Army attacking from the opposite side of the "neck" in order to close it and trap the German divisions within a pocket. The task of the 18th Guards Rifle Corps was to break through the German forward lines of fortifications and cut the Staraia Rusa–Kholm road in the vicinity of the villages of Lekhny, Karkachii, Pesok, and Krivovitsa. This road was a key lateral line of communications behind the German front line. Once we had opened this gap in the German lines, Lieutenant General M. S. Khozin's mobile group of the 1st Tank Army and 68th Army was to develop the offensive in the direction of Stoltsy and Luga, into the deep flank and rear of the German Eighteenth Army encircling Leningrad.

Unfortunately, the Germans anticipated our offensive. Before our offensive began, the Germans withdrew the bulk of their forces and equipment from the Demiansk salient and redeployed them to strengthen the shoulders of the former salient—right where the 18th Guards Rifle Corps offensive was targeted. This movement seemed to have surprised Marshal S. K. Timoshenko, the Northwestern Front's commander, as he underestimated the enemy's possibilities and overestimated the capabilities of our 1st Shock Army.

The 1st Shock Army could not fulfill its task. We managed to cut the Staraia Rusa–Kholm road on the first day of the offensive near the village of Karkachii but could advance no farther due to the enemy's strong resistance. The enemy even launched fierce counterattacks, and we had to defend our meager gains for two weeks. Mobile Group Khozin could not gain operational room to maneuver and to develop the offensive, and found any movement at all extremely difficult due to the slush and bogs. This operation was quickly set aside, and Katukov's 1st Tank Army was withdrawn, entrained, and headed southward. We didn't know at the time that it was headed to Kursk.

Our own combat baptism occurred here, but only the 9th Guards Airborne Regiment from our division, plus one of our antitank batteries, participated in the attack. The rest of our division was held in reserve, in a forest about three kilometers behind the forward edge of battle. For two weeks, those of us in reserve carried shells to artillery batteries in their firing positions. There was no motorized transport whatsoever between the ammunition dumps and the firing positions, while the available horses were wild and untrained.

We remained in these positions until the middle of March 1943. At some point during this period, our division's antitank batteries were consolidated into the 6th Separate [Otdel'ny] Guards Tank Destroyer Battalion, but this battalion remained a constituent part of the 4th Guards Airborne Division.

Then the command arrived to pull out of the front lines and return to the rail line that had brought us to the front. Five airborne divisions—the 2nd, 3rd, 4th, 6th, and 9th Guards—as well as all artillery and engineering units attached to the 1st Shock Army's headquarters were withdrawn from the army with orders to move to central Russia.

We reached the railroad at the Soblago station, not far from Velikie Luki. We were filthy and unwashed. Lice were everywhere. Before sleeping (in huts made from fir branches), we toasted our clothes over a campfire. The lice exploded like little grenades. They brought ammunition cartridges and a new uniform for each soldier to us at the Soblago station, and then we set out for Moscow in rail wagons. At the Khovrino station, we had the opportunity to bathe, received new summer uniforms and gear, and then we set off for Kursk, where the Red armies had created a large salient in the German lines during the previous winter offensive.

We had traveled to within five kilometers of Elets when German bombers suddenly swooped down like ravens upon the rail line. We had few planes to provide air defense. Our commanding officer turned to the left down a branch line toward Kastorniia, and our division and artillery regiment managed to avoid the bombing and reach the village of Kliuchi safely.

It was now the middle of April 1943. People were tilling the fields. We wanted to help them but received the response, "Regulations don't permit it. Appeal to the commissar." The commissar, Kleshchev, was a wise man: "Since the regulations do not permit us to give such orders, then let's simply adopt a decision to conduct a *subbotnik* [Note: labor given freely to the state on days off] to render assistance to the population." In this fashion, we were able to lend a hand to the local field work.

At this point in time, lend-lease vehicles from America were beginning to arrive in large numbers. The Red Army needed more drivers for all these vehicles, so I wound up in a driver instruction course. Within four or five days, the training instructor had to leave, and they left me in his place to teach others how to work with a carburetor. From that point on, I was in fact the instructor. Within two weeks, our vehicles arrived—American Willys jeeps. We drove them around to test them. Thus I became a driver in addition to my gun crew duty, and I transferred to the 3rd Battery of the 6th Separate Guards Tank Destroyer Battalion.

Chapter 2

Kursk

Having suffered a defeat at Stalingrad, the Germans decided to take revenge at a place closer to Moscow: the Kursk salient. In the course of the January and February battles our forces had managed to penetrate the German defenses in this region, in some places up to 150 to 200 kilometers. In this fashion, a large oval bulge formed in the front lines, slightly pinched at the base by German salients from the north in the Orlovsk region, and from the south, near Belgorod. From these two directions, from the southern and northern base of the bulge, the Germans decided to strike a blow, to advance to Kursk, and to trap in this pocket a million-man force of our soldiers. If they had managed to succeed, the path to Moscow would have been open, as we had no other forces at that time on the approaches to Moscow.

Defensive Preparations

In preparation for the German offensive, the Stavka gave the order to create an extensive, multilayered system of defensive fieldworks. Five such bands of fortifications were built, the strongest of which were the first, second, and third belts. Each belt consisted of entrenchments, rifle pits, fire positions for antitank artillery, and in the forward zone there were antitank batteries, antitank rifles, and a heavily mined no-man's-land. Communication trenches connected the defensive belts, and in addition shelters and dugouts for the infantry had been built. The basic plan was that when the German tanks advanced, only the antitank guns and their crews would remain above ground, while the infantry and *avtomatchiki* [submachine gunners] would remain concealed and under cover. When the tank battle concluded, our infantry and *avtomatchiki* would emerge.

The task of the five belts of defense was to destroy the maximum number of enemy tanks, self-propelled guns, and infantry. We wanted to bleed the attacking German armies dry. Once the enemy had spent itself and lost the capability to conduct an offensive, then we would go on the counterattack.

Our antitank battalion was still part of the 4th Guards Airborne Division. Consisting of three batteries of guns towed by American-made Willys jeeps, we served as a mobile antitank reserve for the commander of the 4th Guards Airborne Division's artillery. Our gun was the long-barreled 45-mm antitank gun. I should mention here that our 45-mm cannons were equipped with the PP-9 optical sight, which permitted us to conduct precise fire, almost like a sniper rifle. Thus it was possible to strike any specific spot on a tank out to a range of 500 meters. In other places along the front, there were short-barreled 45-mm guns for use against infantry and other soft targets.

The 4th Guards Airborne was part of the 18th Guards Rifle Corps, under the command of Lieutenant General N. P. Pukhov's 13th Army in Colonel General K. K. Rokossovskii's Central Front. The 13th Army held the northern shoulder of the Kursk bulge. The 18th Guards Rifle Corps held a sector of the front to the east of the key railroad junction Ponyri Station. Our division, the 4th Guards Airborne, was situated near the small villages of Somovo and Nemchinovka, next to the Sosna River. To the west lay the village of Samodurovka.

We were usually positioned about 70 to 100 meters behind the front line, where the infantry and *avtomatchiki* crouched. Any farther back, and we would have been ineffective: our 45-mm guns were too small and weak. However, sometimes it happened that we bounded forward to the front line to fire a round, but then withdrew back again. At Kursk we remained on the defensive constantly, but we had four reserve firing positions.

The Red Army's 9th and 19th Tank Corps were located in this area. At the forward edge of our defenses, their tanks were dug in: only the barrel of the tank's main gun protruded above the earth. Along the forward edge of our defense lines, we had seven tanks per kilometer of front, and 125 antitank guns per kilometer of front. Our Central Front commander, Rokossovskii, wisely decided to concentrate the *front*'s artillery in the region of the anticipated German attack. [Note: The Russian word *front* denotes a Red Army formation equivalent to the "army group" in Western armies, though Soviet armies, and accordingly *fronts,* were smaller than their Western counterparts.] He took half the artillery from the 60th, 65th, and 70th Armies and concentrated them in the 13th Army, and in the 48th Army in the area of Malo-Arkhangel'sk.

We prepared intensively for the German offensive. Whenever there was a lull, our gun crews trained. In the eight-man gun crew, each member had his own role. The weapon commander selects the target, the type of shell, the number of rounds, and gives the order to open fire. The gunner aims the gun and fires the weapon. The breech operator opens and closes the gun's breech in case the automatic device fails. The loader loads the shell into the gun and removes the spent shell casings after firing. The *snariadny* [literally, the "shell man"] prepares the shells for firing and hands them to the loader. What does it mean, to "prepare" the shell? He sets the distance that a shrapnel shell will travel before it explodes. The *iash-chechny* [literally, the "case man"] opens the caissons, wipes the dust from the shells, and so forth. The ammunition carrier carries the shells from the caisson to the gun. The eighth member of the crew is either a driver for horse-drawn guns or the chief mechanic for mechanized towed guns. I was the gunner on my gun crew.

We constantly rehearsed our battle drills so our motions to move, transport, set up and fire our gun became fluid and automatic. But before the offensive, we also trained as regular infantry, so that we could continue to fight in case our gun was knocked out. Our commander conducted regular drills and exercises.

For example, we would crouch some distance from our antitank gun, but under cover. The commander would walk up, grab a forage cap, and toss it high into the air. Then he would shout, "It's a German shell! What do you need to do to protect yourself, so this shell won't kill you?" As the cap began its descent, we would all immediately scatter and hit the ground, with our legs toward the "explosion" and our head covered with our arms, so that if a shell fragment did hit us, it would only strike our legs, while our head would remain intact.

We particularly prepared psychologically to confront German tanks. Once we were marched to a special training ground, with entrenchments facing an open field. In the distance, tanks began rolling toward us. We quickly took shelter in the trenches, and the tanks continued to advance closer and closer. Some comrades became frightened, leaped out of the trenches, and began to run away. The commander saw who was running and quickly forced them back into the trenches, making it clear they had to stay put. The tanks reached the trench line and, with a terrible roar, passed overhead. Here and there, someone might get covered with dirt, or might receive a bruise, but we quickly grasped the idea: it was possible to conceal oneself in a trench from a tank, let it pass right over you, and remain alive. Lie down and press yourself to the bottom of the trench, and shut your eyes. As soon as the tank passes, jump up and toss an antitank mine at its weakly armored rear facing. Those who tried to run away the first time were forced to repeat the exercise until they became accustomed to the noise and sensations of a roaring metal monster passing just overhead.

The command also worked to raise our morale before the coming battle. Everyone spoke openly about how the coming battle might go and tried to prepare psychologically for the fact that it might be even more intense and terrible than we could imagine. There were commissars in our division, who later became deputy commanders in the political sections. We regarded the commissars in different ways: we treated them just as they deserved. We treated our own Commissar Kleshchev kindly. He was a very sincere man, an experienced officer, intelligent and just. During our political lessons and discussion groups, he always spoke to us as if to his own children. But there were also bad political officers, just as there were bad commanders—petty tyrants—if only because there are also good and bad people.

The Red Army also had another way to help boost morale among the soldiers. Litvin said that each man had a daily ration of vodka, which was provided at the morning meal. The quantity was small, only 100 grams, but the troops welcomed this token of support in the form of the national spirit. Normally, according to Litvin, this ration was more the exception rather than the rule, but before and during the battle of Kursk, the vodka ration was a regular daily morale boost.

Our scouts had long been unable to "grab a tongue" [*in Red Army parlance, a living prisoner of war*] in order to ascertain the start date and time of the German offensive. So it happened on the evening of 4 July, Colonel Dzhandzhgava, commander of the 15th "Sivash" Rifle Division,[1] gave the order for a scouting party to go and at whatever cost take a prisoner, so we could learn when the offensive would begin. Our scouts crawled forward in the darkness and came upon a team of German combat engineers in no-man's-land, removing the antitank mines from a minefield. The Germans were placing little flags to indicate the cleared lanes for their tanks to use. Our scouts stealthily surrounded the Germans and opened fire, shooting down almost all the Germans. They managed to capture two of them and dragged them back to divisional headquarters by approximately 1:00 A.M.

The German prisoners were arrogant, saying: "You all have only two hours left to live. Within two hours, all of you—*kaput.*" The Germans said that within two hours, the German artillery preparatory fire would begin, and at 4:00 A.M., their tanks would take the offensive.[2]

Our commanders had prepared ahead of time a plan for a preemptive counterartillery barrage to occur within a half hour of the start of the German preparatory bombardment. The plan was to disrupt the attack by striking known German artillery positions, and troop and tank assembly areas.

Our preparation for this was thorough. Approximately half of our 1,200 artillery pieces in this area of the Kursk bulge were assigned to this counterpreparation fire plan. In general, it was the larger 76-mm and 120-mm artillery guns that took part. Each gun tube had 110 ammunition shells in a regulation combat load [*boekomplekt*], a mixture of armor-piercing, high-explosive, shaped charge, shrapnel, and smoke. We also had small quantities of special antitank shells with tungsten cores. At Kursk before the German attack began, each of our artillery pieces had three such combat loads at every firing position. One load was available for immediate use, while the other two were stored nearby in earthen bunkers.

Our reconnaissance parties had infiltrated German lines to find and mark the location of German batteries on maps. Otherwise, for a short period before the battle's onset, they did not pester them, for they did not want them to change positions.

The Battle Begins and My Wounding

At 2:00 A.M., 5 July 1943, my shift to stand guard over our guns near the village of Nemchinovka had just started. The weather was cloudy, and the night was particularly dark. Suddenly in the distance behind me, I could see the flashes of explosions. I might have surmised that it was our own artillery firing, as we knew that from day to day the offensive could begin. For some reason, though, it seemed to me at first that the German shells were impacting far behind our lines in a strange, linear way, but I couldn't hear the sound of the explosions. If it had been the Germans firing, we would have had shells bursting around us. I thought, "What kind of strange artillery preparatory barrage is this?"

Our counterpreparatory barrage lasted for thirty minutes, and these thirty minutes stunned the Germans and delayed their attack. It required approximately two hours for them to gather their wounded, haul away their damaged vehicles, and reorganize for the attack. Only when they had completed these tasks did they begin their own artillery preparatory fire. Yet our surprise anticipatory barrage must have badly damaged their artillery, for it seemed that they delivered only half the blow to our forward lines that we were anticipating. And in return, now not just 600, but all 1,200 of our guns began to fire in return.

The Germans were concentrating their artillery fire on the sector of our front facing their 20th Panzer Division. Our 15th "Sivash" Rifle Division occupied this sector. Our infantry were taking cover in shelters, but approximately 15 percent of our men died immediately during the German preparatory bombardment. Of course, the shelters could not save everyone: if a shell struck a shelter directly, the people inside died.

After the German artillery preparatory fire, the German tanks advanced, followed by their motorized infantry and submachine gunners. Our infantry remained concealed in their shelters as the Germans approached. The Germans struck our first line and penetrated into the defenses of our forward regiments. Whatever tanks our antitank guns did not manage to knock out, the first-line infantry let pass through their trenches and then assaulted them from behind with antitank mines.

On the first day of battle, the Germans managed to advance 800 meters. But by evening, fierce counterattacks by reserve units forced them to retreat and changed the situation a little. In some places, the Germans had gained 300 meters, in other places they had gained a little farther. But in one way or another, the Germans had nevertheless managed to strike a wedge into our defensive lines.

The fighting had been intense. Near the village of Samodurovka, our 76-mm battery under the command of Captain Igishevo stood.

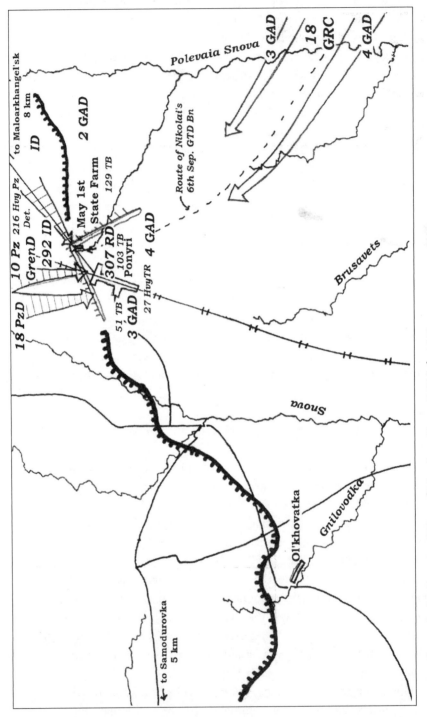

Map 1. The Battle for Ponyri and First of May State Farm, 7–12 July 1943

This battery on the first day destroyed seventeen German tanks during two attacks. At the end of those assaults, of the thirty-two men and four guns in the battery at the start of the battle, only one gun remained undamaged and three men of the battery remained alive. When the Germans attacked a third time, the remaining gun knocked out three more tanks, but a fourth tank crushed the gun and tiny crew under its tracks, destroying the final gun and killing the remaining men. Captain Igishevo was posthumously awarded the title of Hero of the Soviet Union, and since the battle, the village of Samodurovka has been renamed in his honor as Igishevo.

In the first hours of the German offensive, our antitank battalion received the order to advance immediately to the forward edge of the battle, so that by 5:00 P.M., 5 July, my battery arrived in the 307th Rifle Division's sector and was placed under its temporary command. At the divisional headquarters, our battery commander received the order to support one of the division's rifle regiments, which was holding the "Pervomaisk" [First of May] State Farm just to the northeast of Ponyri (see map 1).

Around midnight of 5 July, our battery moved into position to block a section vulnerable to tank attack—a strip of terrain about 800 meters wide lying between two deep, parallel ravines east of Ponyri. The field between the two ravines was covered in uncut rye. We camouflaged our gun positions and established our fields of fire. In every battle, each weapon of our battery had a specific sector of the defensive fire zone allotted to it, which overlapped slightly with the sectors assigned to neighboring guns. This was an effort to ensure that all guns did not select the same target, and tried to reduce the chaos of battle.

The morning of 6 July dawned cloudy, with a low overcast sky that hindered the operations of our air force. Around 6:00 A.M., our position was attacked head-on by a group of approximately 200 submachine gunners and four German tanks, most likely PzKw IVs. The tanks led the way, followed closely by the infantry. The Germans were attempting to find a weak spot in our lines.

The Germans advanced across the uncut rye field directly toward our firing positions, but they didn't seem to see us. We felt a gnawing fear in the pit of our bellies as the German tanks rumbled toward us, stopping every fifty to seventy meters to scan our lines and fire a round. In the general din of battle, we practically could not hear the German shells exploding, but we could see the shells streaking through the air in the direction of our positions. The shells flew harmlessly over our heads, as the Germans hadn't yet spotted us and were targeting likely positions behind us. My knees and legs began to tremble wildly, until we received the command to swing into action and prepared to fire. The shaking stopped, and we became possessed by the overriding desire not to miss our targets.

When the Germans had reached within approximately 300 meters of us, we opened fire at the tanks. Our Number One gun set a tank ablaze with its first shot, and then managed to knock out a second tank. The combined fire of our Number Three and Number Four guns knocked out a third German tank. The fourth tank managed to escape. Since my gun had no tanks in its zone of fire, we opened up on the advancing infantry with fragmentation shells. The German submachine gunners stubbornly continued to push forward. As they drew closer, we switched to shrapnel shells and resumed fire on them. Not less than half the Germans fell to the ground, and the remaining drew back to their line of departure. As we watched the Germans fall back and the one German tank continued to burn, we wanted to leap for joy and shout "Urrah!" at the top of our lungs; such was our happiness at our success.

After we had repulsed this German probe, the sergeant major brought us breakfast, and 100 grams of vodka each to celebrate our victory. We began to eat "American soup"—a puree of peas and chicken meat. As we ate, we didn't particularly notice that the sky was clearing, and that both air forces were beginning to operate.

About 10:00 A.M., a flight of ten Ju-87 "Stukas" suddenly appeared overhead. We called them "Musicians," because of the sound of their air sirens as they dove. These Stukas seemed to have no identified targets but dove upon our lines, and each one released four 50-kg bombs. We took cover, but not a single bomb struck one of our gun pits or bunkers, and there were no losses in our battery.

Within thirty minutes, another flight of "Musicians" appeared and began a new bombing run. This time, they seemed to have located our battery's position, and the first bombs exploded fifty to seventy meters ahead of our guns. The last plane dove directly upon our battery and released its bomb load. One of the bombs flew directly at my dugout. I saw my own unavoidable death approaching, but I could do nothing to save myself: there was not enough time. It would take me five to six seconds to reach a different shelter, but the bomb had been released close to the ground, and needed only one or two seconds to reach the earth—and me.

During these brief seconds as I watched the bomb fall, my entire conscious life flashed through my mind. Everything seemed to happen in slow motion. I badly didn't want to die at the age of twenty. I had a fleeting thought to ask God to spare my life, but then I remembered that I was a Komsomol member, and therefore I couldn't make such a request. Just before the bomb struck, I rolled over facedown in my little trench and covered my face with the palms of my hands. As I was turning my face away, I caught a glimpse of a narrow dust storm, about twelve meters high, moving in my direction. Just as I completed the turn, I heard the bomb explode. There was a repulsive smell of TNT, and I felt two strong blows to my head. It seemed to me that my head must have been torn off. The thought flickered, "How painless it is to die!"

The bomb had exploded very close to my trench, and I was buried in loose dirt. Battery commander Bondarev and some of my comrades frantically dug me out of the earth once the bombing ended. They dragged me out up to my waist and thought that I was dead. They gently raised my head, let it go, and my head dropped back down. I was unconscious. They tried to rouse me three or four times. Then someone gave me a good shake, and I regained consciousness. When I woke up, I remembered the sensation that my head had been torn off and I thought: "Enough. I'm alive."

I began to see things around me, but everything was red. My face was covered with blood. One of my comrades lifted my hand and gave it a shake, and I could see a white color. My hands were bloody. Evidently, blood was pouring from my ears and nose, but I didn't take notice of it. I turned my head and I could see exploding shells in the distance—bright orange columns, and about three or four meters above them, roiling, black clumps of smoke. One explosion, a second, a third—I admired them, and I thought, "How beautiful, just like in the movies." I watched them and I was happy that I was alive, that I could see, and that I could think.

Suddenly I saw one of my comrades starting to run, then a second and a third—the man who had dug me out of my premature grave. I looked up, and I saw above me a dozen more Junkers flying. I thought: "That time I survived, but this time they'll kill me." Somehow I clawed myself free from the loose earth that still covered my legs and hopped out of the trench. I ran toward the approaching Junkers, and I watched to see where the bombs would fall when they released them, to know where to take cover. I ran and ran, then dove into a small pit carved into the ground. The walls of the pit shook from the blast percussions, and I was sprinkled with dirt from above me. I lay there, and I counted: "One, two, three. . . . " Among my other duties, it was my job to count how many bombs fell upon the area of our battery for the after-battle reports. The German bombers normally dropped six, eight, or twelve bombs. They were bombing us with small 50-kg antipersonnel fragmentation bombs. These bombs had a pointed pintle that would stick into the earth. When the bomb exploded, fragments would spray outward, striking everything around and evenly mowing the grass within the blast zone.

The bombing ceased, the walls of the pit stopped shaking, and suddenly I could feel something stirring beneath me. I looked: there was a soldier lying under me. The pit turned out to be one of our communications way stations, a small emplacement for one of our signalmen. A distance of one to one and a half kilometers separated one of these signal stations from the next. It was the signalman's job to lie there with a receiver pressed to his ear, all the while listening: as soon as conversation over the line stopped, it meant the line was broken. That was his signal to climb out of his pit, find the break in the lines, and repair it.

I looked at the signalman, and I could see his lips were moving. I motioned to him that I couldn't hear anything. Only now did I begin to understand that I was deaf. I climbed out of the hole and sat down next to it. The commander of our battery approached me, and by the articulation of his lips I understood that he was asking, "What happened?" I tried to give the answer, "Everything's OK," but when I opened my mouth to speak, my tongue fell out and hung uselessly, and I couldn't pull it back in—another consequence of the concussion.

He took me by the hand, led me to the right seat of his vehicle, and took me to a medical aid station. A doctor examined me there, and wrote out a note for me: "Don't worry—within four to six hours, your tongue will return to its proper place, but do not try to speak without permission from a doctor, or else your tongue may refuse to return back to its proper place." He prescribed a sedative for me and told me, "Your best medicine is time, time, time." We returned to our antitank battalion to recover in our own medical sanitary station. Tumarbekov (who also was concussed by the bombing) and I sat next to the cook and helped clean potatoes and keep the stove burning. That night, about 2:00 A.M., I woke up, and I could feel that my mouth wouldn't close. Inside, it felt like a whole family of hedgehogs had taken residence, because the tongue was hanging, and the pimples on it dried out and began to prickle.

After two or three days, this dried skin began to fall off my tongue. On the third day, my hearing began to return. I could hear the sound of flying bombers. On the fifth day, the doctor permitted me to speak two words, and my hearing began to improve. Within one and a half weeks I was hearing well and speaking with a stutter. By 16–17 July, I returned to my gun crew. It was now no longer at Ponyri but had advanced to the Germans' own starting positions for their offensive.

I always regretted my wounding on 6 July. I was ashamed that I had only fought for two days from the start of the offensive. Our battery remained under the 307th Rifle Division's command until the end of 9 July, when the 4th Guards Airborne Division replaced the 307th Rifle Division's positions at Ponyri and we returned to our own division.

After his wounding and during his convalescence, the fighting continued to rage as Model's 9th Army made strong efforts to penetrate the dense Russian defensive network. Litvin provides a general sketch of this fighting and highlights the role of his division and the antitank units. Unfortunately, his wounding on 6 July prevented us from receiving an eyewitness report to the fighting for Ponyri.

My comrades caught me up on news of the battle and told me about events I had missed. By 8 July, the Germans had made advances everywhere up to twelve kilometers and had occupied Ponyri.[3] Our 4th Guards Airborne Division was brought to Ponyri and told, "You are Guards—you are ordered to halt the Germans here and restore our lines."

On the evening of 8 July, our 7th and 9th Airborne Regiments approached within 600 meters of the Ponyri railway station and prepared to attack. The next morning, 9 July, our regiments went over to the attack and managed to retake the railway station and school in the center of Ponyri Station. They pushed on to the northern edge of Ponyri Station, where they stopped, having reached the day's objective. However, the Germans immediately counterattacked with a tank and panzer grenadier battalion and cut off the 1st Battalion of the 9th Regiment (under the command of Guards Captain A. P. Zhukov). The 1st Battalion chose to make a stand, and swirling combat ensued. Our comrades managed to seize a German antitank battery with six guns. They turned these on the previous owners and destroyed six German tanks.

Almost the entire 1st Battalion died here. Only those who managed to carry off our wounded from the field of battle remained alive. Both Zhukov and his political officer died in the encirclement and posthumously received the title Hero of the Soviet Union. They were the first Heroes in our division. They have since placed a memorial monument there, in 1989.

After 9 July the Germans advanced not a single kilometer farther. For three days we held the German offensive in check and drove out those Germans that had penetrated our lines. On 12 July, our Briansk Front launched a major offensive to the north in the area of Orel, where the Germans held a bulge in our lines similar to the one we held at Kursk. The Soviet offensive caused Model to halt the attacks of the 9th Army, and together with the Briansk Front we began to press the Germans backward. It was at this point that I rejoined my comrades at the front.

Chapter 3

Pursuit

Once the armies of Rokossovskii's Central Front had fought Model's 9th Army to a bloody standstill, they were required to take part in a long-planned Soviet counteroffensive, Operation Kutuzov, against the Orel bulge to the north. The Central Front's right-wing 70th, 13th, and 48th Armies were to attack northward in order to link up with Western Front's 11th Guards Army and assist in trapping three German corps defending the Orel salient. This was a difficult task, as these very same Red armies had suffered heavy losses in stopping Model's thrust and had to reorganize and resupply for offensive operations in just a matter of days. Litvin's account now turns to this phase of the 1943 summer battles, but it is sketchy. Perhaps his memory of these times was hampered by the concussion he had suffered near Ponyri on 6 July.

Operation Kutuzov

Once we had regained our initial positions at the outset of the Kursk battle, on 15 July we went on the offensive toward Kromy, which was a major German supply center for the German forces in the Orel bulge. We advanced together with our neighboring 70th Army of the Central Front, and with the Briansk Front to our right. Our attack was designed to cut off a German group defending Orel.

The going was very hard, and our advance was slow—only two to three kilometers a day. By the time we had pushed the Germans back to their starting lines, the Central Front had lost 40 percent of its personnel. The 15th "Sivash" Rifle Division that had defended Samodurovka suffered enormous losses. But the losses in our anti-tank battalion were light—only Tumarbekov and me. I can explain this only by the fact that the infantry remained in direct contact with the enemy continuously, and died from bullets and shells, or were crushed by tanks or strafed by planes. But our antitank gunners participated in battle only episodically and were protected from bullets and shell fragments by the gun shields.

We advanced past Malo-arkhangel'sk, and there we found an area that had been entirely sown with German graves. Crosses fabricated from white birch marked each grave, and upon each cross hung a German helmet. It seemed that the Germans had buried an entire brigade here. While the fighting had been going on in the area, the Germans had brought their corpses here and buried them. They very, very rarely left behind the bodies of their fallen comrades whenever they withdrew. They always tried to carry them off with them when they retreated, and left them only when the pressure from our advances was unbearable.

I returned to this spot some thirty years after the war and did not find a single trace of this cemetery. Local authorities had destroyed it and established a park in its place. In contrast, the Germans always take care of our graves there, in Germany. At the fiftieth anniversary of Kursk, five German officers came and asked permission to place a monument to their fallen soldiers, without names. When the local authorities asked for our opinion on the matter, we said that we were not opposed to it. But whether or not a monument has been placed there, I don't know.

In general I am not opposed to such monuments, because the average German soldier was only doing his duty. Of course, other Red Army veterans of the war have a different view. I have an acquaintance who fought at Stalingrad. To his disgust, the Germans were allowed to build a monument there to honor their fallen soldiers. So this acquaintance of mine is always saying, "I'm going to drive over there and I'm going to destroy this monument with my own car." I tell him, "Why are you so upset? After all, they were only soldiers, just like us. They tried to riddle you with a machine gun, and you tried to do the same to them. It's just a piece of good luck that you didn't get killed, that they only wounded you."

Our further advance toward Kromy was difficult and slow, as the Germans offered stiff resistance. To indicate the severity of the fighting in Operation Kutuzov, it is necessary only to look at our casualties in the Central Front. Whereas the Central Front suffered 32,000 casualties in the first five days of the Kursk fighting around Ponyri, by the time the Germans had withdrawn from the Orel bulge, our *front* had suffered an additional 118,000 casualties.

Soviet forces liberated Orel on 5 August, the same day that we regained Belgorod from the Germans. In honor of these twin successes, Stalin ordered a celebratory artillery salute in Moscow, the first such one of the war. We did succeed in encircling some of the Germans, but many of them simply fled.

Soon after the Central Front joined the offensive against Army Group Center's salient around Orel, the commanding general of Army Group Center, von Kluge, ordered construction to begin on a line of field fortifications, dubbed the Hagen Line, across the base of the Orel bulge. For once, Hitler did not insist on a rigid defense. Pressed by events elsewhere in Russia and in the Mediterranean, where the Western Allies had landed on Sicily and Mussolini's government in Italy had collapsed, Hitler realized that he needed divisions elsewhere. He decided to shorten Army Group Center's lines by withdrawing from the Orel bulge. On the night of 1 August, Army Group Center's Second Panzer Army and Ninth Army began a fighting withdrawal back to the Hagen Line. The Western, Briansk , and Central Fronts of the Red Army pressed the retreating German forces closely, but their attempt to pocket significant numbers of German forces was hampered by heavy rains, mud, and tough opposition. By 17 August, the German armies had successfully withdrawn to the Hagen Line. A brief pause in the heavy fighting ensued, as the Red Army's Briansk and Central Fronts pulled up before the Hagen position, replenished their units with fresh men and material, and reorganized to resume the offensive.

After we had taken Orel, the front lines were reduced in length, and the *front* commander Rokossovskii began reorganizing his forces. As part of this reorganization, our 18th Guards Rifle Corps was transferred to the 70th Army, which was concentrated in the area of Dmitrovsk-Orlovsk. There we received some replacements and rested, but we soon received the order to march once again. Although we didn't know it at the time, Rokossovskii had decided to send our 18th Guards Rifle Corps to the 60th Army on the extreme left flank of his *front*.

In the darkness, we abandoned our firing positions and concentrated not far from the main thoroughfare. The next morning we fell into order and prepared for the march to the vicinity of Konotop. We set off on the new offensive in the darkness that night. The divisional column moved along the main highway to the southwest. Before morning we turned off the road to the right. We marched approximately four kilometers, and there occupied new firing positions.

Nearby, the sounds of stubborn fighting were audible. The city of Sevsk was somewhere not far away.

The Germans were trying to break through our lines, so our 18th Guards Rifle Corps had been stopped en route to the 60th Army in order to help contain the German attack. For nearly a week, we took part in the repulse of the German counteroffensive. My antitank battalion shifted position at night from sector to sector, sometimes moving as far as ten to fifteen kilometers. During these relocations, we sometimes bumped into our colleagues—the 76-mm gun crews of the 1st Artillery Regiment. It was only then did we realize that not just our 4th Guards Airborne Division but also the entire 18th Guards Rifle Corps had been reassigned to the 60th Army on the front's left flank.

On 26 August, Central Front resumed the offensive against Army Group Center. It concentrated its efforts on the weak German Second Army defending Sevsk and southward to its tenuous connection with Army Group South. The Second Army had been mauled in the fighting in the previous winter and had been neglected since by the German OKH (Oberkommand des Heeres [Army High Command]) for reinforcements or replacements because it had not been assigned an offensive role in Operation Citadel. Second Army was far more vulnerable than Ninth Army to the north, and Rokossovskii's Central Front quickly broke through the German defenses in front of Sevsk. Farther to the south, near Klintsy, Central Front's left-flank army, the 60th, to which the 18th Guards Rifle Corps was headed, quickly punched a hole in the Second Army's line and broke into the German rear.

To counter the Central Front's resumed offensive, von Kluge shifted a panzer division and two infantry divisions from the Ninth Army and threw them into a sharp counterattack northwest of Sevsk on 29 August. On the same day, the 60th Army drove twenty-five miles into the German rear behind the Second Army's south flank. Rokossovskii, who had adroitly maneuvered his forces on the defensive at Kursk, now showed similar ability on the offensive. To reinforce the 60th Army's success, he sent the 18th Guards Rifle Corps to it and then shifted the entire 13th Army, the 61st Army, and the 2nd Tank Army to the left flank. The combined forces severed the German VIII Corps from the rest of the Second Army. More seriously for the Germans, as the triumphant armies of the Central Front continued to advance, they opened a huge gap between Army Group Center and Army Group South, which the German OKH was unable to close.[1] Both army groups' flanks were exposed, and the path southwest to Kiev lay virtually wide open. Second Army tried to screen this gap with two security divisions and a Hungarian division, but they were helpless to stop an advance by three Russian armies.

During this advance, the 60th Army, to which Litvin's unit now belonged, occupied the extreme left flank of the Central Front and moved en echelon to its neighbor on the right, the 13th Army. In this way, the 60th Army served to guard Central Front's left flank from any surprise thrust from Army Group South and was able to cooperate with the Voronezh Front as the Red armies rolled toward the Dnepr River with increasing speed. Litvin's narrative now turns to this heady advance to the Dnepr.

Drive to the Dnepr River

Once the enemy resistance had finally been broken, our division advanced farther to the southwest, in the general direction of Kiev. We bypassed Glukhovo and Krolevets and seized Konotop off the march without any fighting. We reached Bakhmach and somewhere just beyond Bakhmach halted, just before dawn. In Bakhmach, we had captured approximately twenty of Vlasov's soldiers, Russians who had gone over to the other side.

Battery commander F. Nishchakov, who had recently replaced Senior Lieutenant Bondarev, went to the artillery regiment's headquarters to receive orders, and while we waited, those of us who were sitting dropped to sleep on the spot. Captain Nishchakov returned with combat orders. The battery was supposed to support a new advance by protecting against possible enemy tank counterattacks. Before dawn, we were ordered up to the line of departure, to the village of Sambor.

We reached the outskirts of Sambor and stopped, just as dawn began breaking. A Ukrainian woman emerged from the nearest hut and told us that the Germans had left Sambor on horse-drawn carts just ten minutes before us. In agitation, she further said that two German stragglers had just dropped by her home to steal eggs and milk. She pointed out which direction they had taken, and some of our boys took off in pursuit, overtook the offenders, and killed the lovers of eggs and milk right on the spot.

At that moment an observer reported that he had spotted the enemy's retreating carts. The battery commander gave the command to the Number One gun to destroy the enemy unit. After three rounds, the horses of three of the carts had been killed. The other three carts were abandoned, the soldiers running for cover. The battery commander ordered up two vehicles to go to the carts. Up to eight people got into each vehicle, and we set off. Around the carts we found three dead German soldiers and two wounded. Nishchakov ordered battery section commander Lieutenant Seliutiny and Sasha Kornilov, driver for the first gun team, to take eight men and set off in pursuit of the Germans who had escaped. We, however, remained with the carts. The pursuit detachment caught up with the Germans, who opened fire upon their pursuers in resistance. But our boys surrounded them and wiped them out. From the captured carts we took everything that could prove useful in camp life and battle.

After the destruction of the German supply cart train, Guards Colonel Nikolaev, the commander of the division's artillery, arrived. Captain Kleshchev, the division's commissar, or, in his new title, deputy commander of the division's political department, also appeared by our guns.

We hooked up our guns again and resumed the advance. We traveled the very same road upon which the German cart train had recently been destroyed. We passed the wounded horses and the wrecked carts, then the corpses of the Germans who had tried to offer resistance, and continued to the southwest.

Gaivoron

We drove slowly. We often stopped, so that we could carefully examine the terrain ahead of us. We were alone—there were no rifle detachments either ahead of us or beside us. Our battery consisted of four 45-mm guns, approximately forty men, thirty-five PPSh submachine guns, and one German machine pistol, not counting pistols and grenades. Yet we were leading the advance![2] My own Willys led the small column. Colonel Nikolaev rode with me, together with my gun crew. The other officers of the battery and division rode in the following vehicles.

That afternoon we approached the village of Golenok. We stopped on a low hill short of the village, which lay peacefully below us in a shallow valley. We examined the surroundings through binoculars, then unhooked our guns and turned them toward the village. We prepared for battle and sent a scout party forward to the village. Guards Captain Kleshchev commanded the scout detachment. The village turned out to be empty of enemy soldiers, and the scouts gave the signal, "Clear."

We drove into the village cautiously and slowly, observing the same distance of 100 to 150 meters between vehicles. We stopped on opposite sides of the street. Lieutenant Seliutin set off with the gun crew leaders to select firing positions for our guns. Local inhabitants began to approach us. The first were two young adolescent boys around twelve to thirteen years of age. They stared at us, and then asked, "Are you Soviets or Germans?" We told them, "We are soldiers of the victorious Red Army." The young lads began to jump up and down, and cried out to their fellow villagers. Three old men walked up to us and began to look us over. We were all wearing shoulder straps, and the officers had little stars upon theirs. In occupied territory, few people knew that such insignia and signs of rank had been reintroduced into the army of the proletariat!

Deputy political officer Guards Captain Kleshchev gathered together the villagers and began to tell them about the situation on the front and in the country. Battery commander Nishchakov and Colonel Nikolaev were obtaining useful intelligence about the enemy: where the Germans were situated, how many had left, and so forth. The SMERSH[3] head was making inquiries, seeking to identify accomplices to the Germans.

We set up our guns in their firing positions. Half of each gun crew kept watch over the guns. The remaining combed the village under the command of the captain of the Special [counterintelligence] Department. Colonel Nikolaev and Captain Nishchakov were deciding what to do next. The day's objective for the advance was the village of Gaivoron.[4] Eight to ten kilometers remained to reach it. All day we had advanced without halting. It was now 5:00 P.M., and our stomachs were growling. The villagers brought us food and even potent *samogon* [Russian moonshine], but we didn't drink any: we were still on duty and standing in firing positions.

After spending two hours in our firing positions, we began to ask the artillery commander for permission to continue on to Gaivoron. There were no audible sounds of combat nearby, which we used to support our argument. Moreover, we wanted to prepare a nice dinner and manage to eat it before the 9th Regiment's main forces moved up. The colonel turned aside our solicitations. Within several minutes, a cavalry squadron suddenly appeared. The artillery commander ordered them to reconnoiter the enemy in Gaivoron.

About forty-five minutes after the cavalry squadron departed on their assigned task, the commander of our gun crew, Guards Sergeant Korol'kov, and I again requested permission to advance the battery to Gaivoron. The colonel relented and granted our request; the day was winding to an end, and we could move forward until we met our advance scouts, the cavalry squadron.

We limbered our guns and prepared to leave. But now we discovered that one of the tow vehicles had broken down. The gun crew, under the leadership of Guards Captain Kleshchev, remained behind in the settlement to serve as a garrison. They were ordered to defend the village in case of an enemy attack.

The remaining three guns went ahead. We passed a railway crossing and turned onto the road that led to Gaivoron. We still had approximately 5 kilometers left to reach the town. We were traveling quietly, with a separation of about 100 meters between vehicles. Our cannons were prepared for action, the muzzle covers removed. We moved on but still saw no trace of the cavalry squadron that had preceded our march. We passed a windmill, and now only about a kilometer remained between Gaivoron and us.

The colonel ordered us to stop and hide behind a haystack on the left side of the road. We took cover and waited for the cavalry. It was silent, and there was no sign of anyone. By evening, the colonel permitted the battery commander to move into Gaivoron. The order of movement was as follows: distance—100 meters between cars; silent travel, all weapons at hand and grenades prepared; no coughing or smoking.

Our jeep took the lead. The colonel and the SMERSH captain rode with us. I laid my machine pistol on the hood of the truck. We moved along past tilled fields until we reached the first huts on the outskirts of Gaivoron. It was now twilight. We stopped and remained in our seats. From behind the gate of a neighboring courtyard, a woman emerged. She looked at the stars on our shoulder straps and recognized that we were Russian. She threw up her arms: "What are you going to do? The town is full of Germans!" The colonel asked for more details, and her husband, who had just returned from the center of town, explained the situation to him. While they went inside the couple's home to speak, we were ordered to unhook our guns and take up positions at the nearby crossroads. The gun crews made the guns ready to fire, while we, the drivers, carried ammunition boxes to them. I brought up five boxes of fragmentation, one box of armor piercing, and two boxes of shrapnel shells.

The local resident told the officers that approximately 400 German supply wagons were standing in the town square. In a garden about 300 meters away from us were three small cannons, their barrels pointed in our direction; but he had seen no tanks or heavy weapons.

Within about fifteen minutes, in the fading light we began to make out the supply wagons' horses not far away, and we could hear unhurried German conversation. The spotters carefully observed what was happening in their respective sectors, while the rest of each crew prepared for battle. Half of each crew remained by their weapon, while the remaining men took up security positions around each gun.

Two of our 45-mm cannons were aimed toward the center of the town, with the enemy's 37-mm guns and the main force of hostile troops within their field of fire. Our third gun was turned at a ninety-degree angle from the other two and was covering the approach along the road upon which we had traveled. We concealed our vehicles behind a house, which was enclosed by a wattle fence. We drivers were supposed to guard approaches to the battery's firing positions from the rear.

The senior ranking officer among us was a certain Captain Antipenko, an officer in the Special Department. Once our vehicles had been concealed and we had occupied our firing positions, I went up to the captain and requested his permission to join the others at the firing position with my captured German light machine gun. I had carried this weapon, and two cans of ammunition belts (500 cartridges) for it, ever since we had left Ponyri, but I had no occasion yet to try it out in battle. The captain gave me his permission to take up a fighting position and wait for the enemy or for further orders.

Once he had clarified the situation, Colonel Nikolaev ordered us to take up an all-round defense and wait for the approach of the 9th Regiment's forces following behind us. We were ordered to initiate battle only once the main forces had arrived. Colonel Nikolaev ordered our battery commander, Nishchakov, to send his orderly to the commander of the airborne regiment behind us, in order to explain the situation to him and hasten the regiment's departure for Gaivoron. Colonel Nikolaev sent platoon leader Lieutenant Seliutin to accompany the orderly and ordered the driver of the first gun crew, Sergeant Sasha Kornilov, to take them in his vehicle.

By now it was fully twilight, and then it became completely dark. Near midnight, Lieutenant Seliutin returned from the regiment, and together with him arrived a major (the regiment's operations officer), two more officers, a radio operator, and two *avtomatchiki*. They held a meeting and decided to attack the enemy that night. The signal for the attack would be a volley from our guns.

A little after midnight, we could hear the soft clanking of mess tins approaching from the rear, along the road upon which we had traveled that day. Several of the airborne troops had carelessly attached their mess tins, and as they marched, the tins rattled against their sapper shovels or the handles of their Finnish knives. We understood that the main body of the regiment was approaching, but the Germans also heard the noise and were now alert, though they seemed to be caught off guard.

Our infantry had managed to reach within fifty meters of us, when suddenly a German heavy machine gun opened up and fired a long, blind burst. Our men scattered off the road and began to maneuver into attack positions to the left and right, while a few remained in the roadside ditches to divert the Germans' attention and draw their fire.

The reinforcing infantry turned out to be the forward detachment [*peredovoi otriad*] of a battalion that had been following us, but the remaining forces of the regiment were still some distance behind. When the elements of the forward detachment had reached their starting lines for the attack, Colonel Nikolaev gave the command to the battery to open fire. Primarily, we aimed our guns at the garden, where the enemy had deployed their 37-mm guns. The noise of our first shots had not yet died away when the battery commander suddenly rushed to the enemy's supply carts and led back to our position a pair of horses. He tied them up to my vehicle and took off running again.

Our fire and the automatic weapon bursts of the parachutists stunned the Germans, many of whom seemed to be asleep. The

first fifteen minutes of the battle, we had no losses, but gradually
the enemy came to their senses and organized resistance. By the
flashes of our guns, the Germans located our positions and quite accurately blanketed them with fire from their 37-mm guns. While we
bandaged our wounded, we continued this gun duel with the Germans. After ten to twelve minutes of battle, we had nobody killed,
but many in our gun crews were wounded.

We were left with insufficient crew to man two of the guns. At
the third gun, only the crew's driver and the breech operator, Sergeant
Piotr Goriachikh, remained uninjured. At the second gun position,
only the gun's commander, Sergeant Korol'kov, and I remained,
while only the driver Sasha Kornilov remained at the first gun.

By now, the fighting had moved into the center of Gaivoron, and
the need for our cannons had declined. The battery commander
ordered us to withdraw our guns from their fighting positions and
conceal them where our vehicles were parked. This we did. We sent
our wounded to the rear, and now there remained only four of us:
the battery commander Nishchakov, the commander of the second
gun Sergeant Korol'kov, breech operator Goriachikh, and me.

At 2:00 A.M., additional elements of the leading battalion from the
airborne regiment trailing us reached Gaivoron. Once again, the Germans opened fire on them with a heavy machine gun. The regiment's
artillery commander ordered us to suppress the German machine gun.

Sergeant Korol'kov invited me to join him on a reconnaissance
foray. It was necessary to select a new firing position and the route
of approach to it. I managed to determine the machine gun's fire
pattern: short and long bursts would continue for two to three
seconds, and then there would be twenty-five to thirty seconds of
break in the fire. Then the pattern would repeat itself. The tracers
from this machine gun flew past us about twenty meters away. We
selected a new firing position at one of the nearest crossroads. We
could reach the position in our jeep through the kitchen garden of
the outlying farmstead and then manhandle the gun into place by
hand from the farmstead's courtyard. This we decided to do.

Sergeant Korol'kov waited for me in the courtyard, while I returned to my jeep, started up the engine, and brought it up to the
road. I stopped, waiting to hear the next burst from the machine
gun, after which I could cross the fire-swept road. The machine gun
chattered and then fell silent. Before my jeep's headlights, a stream

of red and green tracers flew past and then died out. I started at low speed and kept the engine turning over, so that the engine wouldn't die as I crawled across the roadside ditches. The Germans couldn't hear the sound of my engine, as German shells were bursting not far from where I was headed, and a noisy exchange of automatic fire was occurring. Light from the windows of neighboring homes illuminated my path.

Just as I crawled out of the jeep, I heard the howl of an incoming shell. I quickly took scant shelter under the roof of a nearby home. The gun commander fell flat to the ground behind the shield of the gun. The shell exploded about fifteen meters away. Fragments knocked out the windows of the little house where I was standing, while three fragments penetrated the wall above my head, and I was dusted with chalk and clay. I examined my jeep. It was intact. We unhooked the gun and released the lower half shields, so they would protect our legs in case there was a sudden burst of machine-gun fire as we moved the gun into its firing position.

We rolled the gun to the opposite corner of the crossroads. Korol'kov remained with the gun to prepare it for battle, while I returned to the jeep for ammunition. I chose a case of fragmentation shells and carried it to the road. There I tied a piece of German telephone cable to the case and dashed across the road with the other end of the cable. In that fashion, we dragged the ammunition chest, tumbling, across the road to the gun's position. We loaded the cannon and prepared other shells for firing.

The machine gun lit up with another burst. Crouching behind the gun shield, bullets didn't frighten us. The gun commander immediately caught the gun flashes of the machine gun in the crosshairs of our gun and pressed the trigger. The gun roared. I watched the gun's breech moving in recoil toward me until it reached its limit. The breech opened, and with a ringing sound out flew the empty shell casing, from which curled a whitish puff of smoke. In place of the ejected casing, I quickly loaded another round. The breech shut with a characteristic click, and the barrel returned to its proper position along the tracking. I shouted: "Normal recoil!" and another shot erupted from the barrel, then another, and a fourth. After the seventh shot, we paused and observed the results of our work. Korol'kov had been on target. I counted off the seconds to myself: 25, 30, 45, 75. The enemy machine gun was silent.

We had three rounds left for the gun. Although the enemy machine gun remained silent, the gun commander ordered the remaining rounds to be placed on the same target. I loaded, and the gun fired, until we had exhausted all ten rounds of ammunition. Korol'kov stood watch, while I collected all the spent shell casings and placed them in the ammunition chest. We had to turn them over to supply, or else things would be bad for us. I found nine of the empty casings, but the tenth escaped my initial rapid search.

Three to five minutes passed, and still the enemy machine gun was quiet. The gun commander set off to report to the battery commander that his order had been fulfilled, while I remained with the gun and continued searching for the tenth casing. I found it in the roadside ditch about seven meters from the cannon. The sergeant returned, and we returned to our former position, behind the wattle fence at the rear of the farmstead. The battle receded into the depth of the village. The artillery commander and all the officers who were directing the battle decided to draw up closer to the fighting. Colonel Nikolaev asked the battery commander to give him a man to serve as an orderly. Sergeant Korol'kov was chosen and left with the officers.

There remained three of us, with three guns, around 300 rounds of ammunition, and one jeep with a half tank of fuel. It began to grow light. The enemy's resistance began to increase.

The battery commander ordered us to take up a new firing position on a low elevation, which was around 250 meters north of our current position. We brought up one gun and established its firing position. I carried up eight chests of shells. We placed the remaining two guns and our jeep in a small hollow about 70 meters from our firing position. We set up the first gun and dug in. Then we oriented ourselves and prepared the ammunition: one chest of armor piercing, one of armor-piercing incendiary, two of shrapnel, and ten boxes of fragmentation shells. Once we had completed our preparations for battle, the battery commander allowed us to rest, while he himself set out for a nearby position of 82-mm mortars and howitzers.

When he returned, he told us that the mortars and howitzers had only twelve to sixteen shells remaining per barrel. We had nearly three full daily allotments of ammunition left. The commanders made arrangements: if the enemy approached us closely, we would fire upon them and force them to hug the earth. After this, the mortars would lay down a sheaf of fire and destroy the enemy where they lay. A sheaf of fire is a way of striking a location, so that the shells fall in an overlapping pattern of fragmentation zones. As a result, no piece of ground is left untouched by fragments, and it is impossible for a man to remain intact.

The sun rose in the sky. The sound of battle was audible somewhere on the southern outskirts of the village. The first to stand watch was Sergeant Goriachikh. The battery commander and I lay down under the gun carriages we had concealed in the hollow and immediately fell asleep.

Around noon, it was my turn to stand watch at the observation post. For about thirty minutes, everything remained peaceful. Our neighbors to the right, the artillerists of the regimental howitzers, had not dug in their guns. They were clearly visible. At around 2:00 P.M., bullets began to whistle past our position. I hid behind the gun shield and began to search for the source of the fire. I spotted no one in front of me. Then a bullet flew right past my head, and I could determine the direction of its flight. I looked to the left, where the windmill was located, and began to watch it closely. When we were approaching Gaivoron the evening before, this windmill had been to our right, and nobody had fired at us from it. Evidently, at some point during the night while we were preparing to evacuate our wounded, the Germans had managed to infiltrate into our rear area. We had received word during the night that the Germans had occupied the railroad crossing we had passed over that morning, so when the vehicles with the wounded prepared to depart, I had given my captured German light machine gun and two banks of cartridges to the small convoy's escort.

Now closely examining the windmill, I noticed a puff of rifle smoke, and another bullet whistled past us. Someone was shooting from the windmill's shaft. Having noticed a second shot from the same location, I reported to the battery commander. When two more bullets flew by us, he gave the order to turn our gun to the left and to load it with fragmentation shells. We loaded it, and the battery commander fired three rounds at the windmill.

The first shot knocked off the roof of the windmill, and after the third shot, the windmill's rotary tower collapsed. In order to ensure the elimination of the Germans who had occupied the windmill, the battery commander fired two incendiary rounds at the rubble, which burst into flames.

Within about forty minutes I noticed that some people were moving about under the cover of some bushes in a ditch to our front. Through binoculars, I could see that they were German sub-machine gunners. The ditch offered them excellent cover from rifle or machine-gun fire, and they were gathering force there. I reported this to the battery commander, who gave the command to prepare for battle. We readied shrapnel and fragmentation shells, and I my-self began to keep watch over the Germans through the 45-mm gun's optical sights.

The ditch lay approximately 500 meters from us. After a short period of observation, battery commander Nishchakov ordered me to run to our neighbors on the right, the men manning the mortars and howitzers, and explain the situation to them. By the time I re-turned to my gun, officers from the neighboring units were already there, finishing their discussion of how they would cooperate in the coming battle. The hostile infantry were not yet near, so we had time to prepare all our weapons and grenades. We weren't worried for ourselves: we had around 150 fragmentation and 30 shrapnel shells. To destroy 100 Germans, we had enough ammunition. As we prepared, the German submachine gunners formed up in the ditch, and then in a wave began moving toward us.

The Germans came on, not firing, with submachine guns in their hands and grenades strapped to their bootlegs. Our battery com-mander Nishchakov himself sat behind the gun's sights and directed its fire. He waited until the Germans had advanced fifty meters from the ditch. He opened fire and with the first shot killed a German of-ficer. The German submachine gunners, turning at the sound of the shell explosion, seemed bewildered: there was smoke, but no crater nor officer. The shell had struck the officer in the chest and blown him to pieces, but left no crater on the ground.

Nevertheless, the Germans continued to press their attack. Nishchakov fired three more rounds. They exploded at both ends and in the center of the line of Germans. Up to ten Germans fell dead. The battery commander selected a compact bunch of Ger-mans, aimed at the man in the middle, and fired a shell that hit him in the chest. The explosion struck all those bunched around him.

After these three explosions, the German submachine gunners be-gan to run forward in a crouch and opened fire. We increased the pace of our fire. The Germans began to disperse. Under the explosions of our shells, the submachine gunners ran forward for another thirty seconds or so. We managed to fire twenty-five rounds at them. The Germans dropped to the earth. Nishchakov began shooting at clusters of them, and we fired another twenty shells. When there were no longer any noticeable lines of Germans, we ceased fire. Then the mortar men kicked into action and laid down a sheaf of fire, up to three shells per tube. The field of battle began to darken.

After the mortar attack, five to seven minutes passed, and then the Germans once again rushed forward, although their numbers were now fewer. One German constantly kept turning back to the advancing line, waving his pistol and shouting something. Nishchakov took careful aim, and the leader fell. The others dropped to the ground again. They were now about 300 meters short of our position. They fired their submachine guns, but I didn't hear the bullets, probably because I was paying no attention to them. I brought up ammunition chests and prepared the shells for firing. Goriachikh loaded the gun and kept watch over the recoil. Battery commander Nishchakov aimed the gun and fired it.

The Germans lay in their current positions around ten minutes, and our cannon fell silent. They, perhaps, thought that we had exhausted our ammunition and began to gather in small groups of two to three men, in order to gather up the wounded and carry them to cover back in the ditch. When a half dozen of such groups had appeared, we again opened fire and broke up five of them. The remaining uninjured Germans dropped the wounded and began to pick their way to the haystack, behind which we had hid the day before when we were moving toward Gaivoron. Approximately fifteen submachine gunners took cover behind the haystack. We couldn't take them out there, so we fired a few incendiary rounds at the haystack, but the stack refused to catch fire. Suddenly we saw a German motorcyclist emerge from the village and move toward the haystack. Since the battery commander wasn't aiming at him, he managed to reach the haystack safely and hid behind it. Nishchakov ordered the gun to be loaded with armor-piercing rounds, and fired at the haystack. Then, with fragmentation rounds, we at last managed to torch the haystack.

By evening a battery of 76-mm guns drove up from the 1st Guards Artillery Regiment, under the command of Lieutenant Colonel Kachin. Only now did we sense our extreme fatigue and hunger.

Our colleagues from the artillery regiment quickly prepared their guns for battle and began firing volleys at unseen targets. We meanwhile prepared our three 45-mm guns for movement. This took us about an hour. Soon a ZIS-5 truck from our division drove up, and to it we attached two of our guns. The other we hooked to my jeep.

We returned along the very same road we had taken the day before, only now the windmill was demolished. We reached our destination before nightfall and were greeted as heroes. Among those who met us were our wounded comrades from the night before. The majority of them wanted to remain with the artillery battalion and had refused hospitalization.

Crossing the Dnepr River

The Germans defending Gaivoron withdrew, and we liberated the village of Ich'nia the following day, 18 September. At this point, the German resistance seemed to crumble, perhaps due to their losses in men and material in the recent fighting. Our advance increased its pace. At this point, the Voronezh Front lagged behind us by seventy kilometers.

For a week we moved from flank to flank, supporting the airborne troops wherever necessary with our small firepower. Our successes in the recent battles had dulled our sense of fear. We were confident that our shrapnel shells would lead us to victory in battle.

Not far from the city of Bobrovitsa, our battery received the order to clear the way for the paratroopers in the forward detachment, who were being blocked by self-propelled guns[5] and heavy-caliber machine guns. Upon receiving this assignment, Nishchakov and Seliutin conducted a reconnaissance. We quickly moved into the front line, detached our cannons, and deployed them without digging in. The enemy spotted us and began to fire their machine guns at our positions. We were saved by the fact that our guns were already in their firing positions with their gun shields lowered in place, and the gun crews were crouched behind the shields. Battery commander Nishchakov ordered each gun to open rapid fire at the German self-propelled guns and machine-gun positions. The third gun crew quickly set its target vehicle alight, while our target retreated under cover. Our remaining guns fired at the machine guns. With one self-propelled gun blazing, and the other one falling back, the enemy's machine-gun fire weakened. The commander of the forward detachment led his men forward, while we limbered up our guns. The battery commander began to collect battle reports from the section commanders. It turned out that in the second section, the ammunition carrier Egorov was wounded. Egorov moonlighted as our battery's cobbler, so we were all concerned about his injury! But Egorov refused to go to the hospital, and just as I did after my wounding near Ponyri, he convalesced in the divisional kitchen.

Our 4th Guards Airborne Division resumed its march and headed toward Kiev, but along the way the town of Priluki lay to our right. This town held a German garrison, and we were reluctant to advance farther and leave these Germans behind us. Therefore, we received permission to halt our offensive toward Kiev for twenty-four hours and to liberate Priluki. Each regiment in the division formed a mobile detachment for this purpose, and the batteries in our artillery battalion were parceled out, one to each regiment. My battery was assigned to the 9th Regiment. By evening we had seized Priluki. Each one of our guns had up to 110 shells, and we easily destroyed several German trucks, armored personnel carriers, and a self-propelled gun. That evening the 42nd Guards Division, which had been assigned to liberate Priluki, arrived to find us already in possession of the town, and we set out for Kiev.

We thought we would just march into Kiev and be part of its liberation, but as we neared that city, our columns were redirected toward the village of Domantovo, which lay on the west bank of the Dnepr River about sixty kilometers north of Kiev (see map 2). Our division concentrated all its elements here, in the cover of some woods on the opposite shore, and we prepared to force a crossing. The Germans held the western bank of the river, which was high and overlooked the gently sloping eastern bank of the river.

Although the route to Kiev lay open for Rokossovskii's 60th Army, the Stavka thought the city was too difficult to take by direct assault, so it ordered the 60th Army to redirect its march to the northwest, where the Central Front's 13th Army had already captured several small bridgeheads across the Dnepr north of Kiev, in the vicinity of where the Pripiat' River flows into the Dnepr from the west. According to the Stavka's ambitious plans, Rokossovskii's 13th and 60th Armies were to cooperate in the encirclement

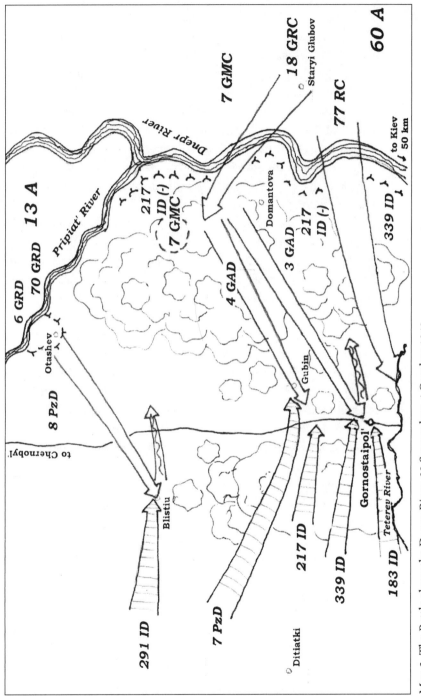

Map 2. The Battle along the Dnepr River, 30 September–4 October 1943

of Kiev from the north, while Vatutin's armies advanced out of the Bukrin bridgehead across the Dnepr to the south of Kiev.

For this plan to succeed, it was important for the Central Front to take and hold bridgeheads across the Pripiat' River, which flows into the Dnepr River and served as a barrier to a turning movement against Kiev by any forces located north of its confluence with the Dnepr. The 13th Army had accomplished this task by 25 September, when the 17th Guards Rifle Corps had seized one bridgehead across the Pripiat' River at Otashev, and the 6th Guards Rifle Division's 70th Guards Regiment had seized another small bridgehead near Domantovo. The Stavka wanted to reinforce this small bridgehead and secure it against German counterattacks, so it could serve as a springboard for the operation to take Kiev.

Accordingly, the Stavka ordered the 60th Army's 18th Guards Rifle Corps, including the 4th Guards Airborne Division, to force a crossing of the Dnepr just to the south of the 70th Guards Regiment's position near Domantovo.[6] Further, the 18th Guards Rifle Corps was to advance and seize the fortified villages of Gubin and Ditiatki.

The task was difficult. At this point, the Dnepr River is 500 to 700 meters wide, with a depth in places of 6 to 8 meters. Elements of the Fourth Panzer Army's LIX Army Corps were still defending this stretch of the Dnepr. A history of the 4th Guards Airborne Division notes that a dominating elevation, marked 115.4 on the military maps, overlooked the Dnepr River at the designated crossing place and covered the approaches to both Gubin and Ditiatki. Given the task to force the crossing and capture this elevation, the 4th Guards Airborne Division's 15th Guards Airborne Regiment's commander, Lieutenant Colonel Birenboim, decided against a direct assault and opted to make two smaller crossings north and south of the German-held hill.[7] Litvin describes one of these crossings.

The 15th Airborne Regiment received the orders to select an assault group to force a crossing of the Dnepr on the night of 29–30 September. Lieutenant Colonel Birenboim selected a company of approximately 100 men under the command of Lieutenant G. F. Bastrakov. Since not all of the soldiers were able to swim (some of the men had just returned from the hospital, while others were new reinforcements), they built three large rafts and mounted machine guns on them.

As soon as it grew dark on the night of 29 September, Bastrakov's assault company quietly set off. They reached the middle of the river and were 150 meters from the opposite bank when a German sentry noticed something and fired a signal rocket. Two illumination flares quickly lit up the river, and the Germans could see our small flotilla. The Germans began firing at the rafts. Bastrakov knew that half the men under his command didn't know how to swim, but nevertheless ordered, "Everyone into the water!" Everyone leaped overboard. While those who didn't know how to swim grabbed onto the sides of the rafts, others began swimming to the far shore. The Germans saw the empty rafts beneath the flickering light of the flares and thought they had wiped out all the Russians. The illumination flares died away, and the German positions fell silent.

When our men had reached the far bank, they quietly formed up, and Bastrakov passed the order for the men to strip to their underwear. He didn't want them to be encumbered by wet, heavy uniforms during the action that lay ahead. The men dropped their overcoats and uniform jackets, grabbed their submachine guns, and began stealthily climbing up the slope. The Germans fired another illumination rocket; our troops gave a ringing "Ura!" and surged forward into battle. The Germans reacted as if they were seeing ghosts and were clearly stunned by the sudden onset of these "apparitions" in white underwear. Our troops rushed into the German entrenchments and shot down nearly all the enemy, even those who tried to escape. Our airborne soldiers in their skivvies smashed the Germans, then returned to the riverbank, retrieved their clothes from their hiding places, and got dressed. For his actions in forcing the Dnepr River, Bastrakov was awarded the title Hero of the Soviet Union.[8]

Immediately, our sappers began building a planked bridge across the Dnepr River just beneath the surface of the water, to hide it from German reconnaissance planes. Next to it they constructed a 400-meter pontoon bridge. The Germans attacked the visible pontoon bridge, but the underwater bridge remained unmarked and unnoticed.

By dawn, the regiments of our division were pouring across these bridges and expanding the bridgehead across the Dnepr. As we waited our turn to cross, our battalion received an order to release one Willys jeep and driver to the command of the 9th Guards Airborne Regiment. Nishchakov selected me.

Chapter 4

I Become a Chauffeur

I said good-bye to my comrades and set out in my jeep to find my new unit. In the town of Oster, they told me that the 9th Guards Airborne Regiment was already across the Dnepr, somewhere opposite Stary Glybov. To reach the Dnepr crossing here, I followed an off-road track that had been literally ground into the sandy soil by the tires and tracks of all the combat vehicles and supply trucks that had preceded me. My powerful and mobile all-terrain Willys churned its way through the loose soil with a howl, and it kept slipping and skidding until I reduced the air pressure in its tires.

I crossed the Dnepr River on an underwater bridge. It had been laid approximately twenty centimeters lower than the water level. The opposite bank of the river was even sandier, but here the sand had been planted with a coniferous forest. The sand wasn't as loose, because someone's caring hands had at one time planted many coniferous saplings.

I arrived at the regimental command post by the end of the day. I found it in a mixed forest of pines and oaks. Everyone greeted me warmly, except for the regimental commander, who was unhappy that he had been forced to wait three days for a vehicle. Scattered around the command post were almost all the regiment's special units: an engineer detachment, a scout platoon, a headquarters' guard platoon of submachine gunners, the regiment's medical and sanitary elements, the supply unit, et cetera.

My service began with digging a dugout for the Willys. I had been assigned to the regimental headquarters' mechanized team. It consisted of the commander, Guards' Senior Lieutenant Kozak; Senior Sergeant Slava (I forget his last name; he was a motorcyclist, but he didn't have a motorcycle); and a driver for the ZIS-5 truck, Ivanov, whose truck was a genuine rolling ammo dump. In the back of the truck were mortar rounds and machine gun cartridges, hand grenades and 50-mm mines, a few general explosives—in general, a complete ammo dump! I was the fourth member of the team, and the fifth—a gunsmith. We were given a small but comfortable earthen dugout as our quarters. It was covered, so that in case of

German shelling, hardly any sand even sprinkled down on us. The place lacked for nothing.

That evening over dinner, as the newcomer, I was the center of attention. The commander carefully studied my certificate, where it had been indicated: "Authorized to drive foreign models."

While forcing the Dnepr River the 9th Guards Airborne Regiment had suffered heavy losses. Now it was basically in a defensive posture and conducted battles of only local significance designed to improve its positions. The regiment was particularly short of active-duty infantry, so virtually the entire regimental artillery was on the front line with the infantry and ready to fire over open sights, since the surrounding terrain was forested.

A Close Call

My second day with my new regiment passed quietly. I improved the car's dugout shelter, camouflaged it, and then dug a little trench next to it for myself. When the day was winding down, I was summoned to the regimental headquarters. I was ordered to be ready and to prepare my Willys for midnight departure for the front lines. Some regimental senior officer wanted to visit a battalion in order to hand out medals and honors for the assault crossing of the Dnepr and the enlargement of the bridgehead. Around 11:00 P.M. I parked my car by the entrance to the headquarters' shelter. Out stepped a Guards major and a sergeant. Both, in addition to pistols, were carrying a PPSh submachine gun and a spare cartridge drum. The major had a waterproof cape draped around his shoulders.

We drove along a little forest road toward the forward lines about one kilometer, then stopped at the edge of the woods. The major and sergeant set off for the battalion, while I remained with the Willys to await their return. Before leaving, the major warned me that our defenses here were very weak, and that German scouts could easily infiltrate. Therefore, he advised me to keep the Willys idling, and for me to keep a sharp watch on the surroundings.

A young pine forest was growing to the right of the road. The diameter of the tree trunks was no thicker than the span of a hand. On the opposite side of the road, a young oak forest was growing. I turned the jeep around, pointing it back toward the command post, and then put it into idle. I took out my pistol and laid it beside my jacket on the seat next to me. I placed my captured German machine pistol on top of the jacket and began to listen. It was quiet, and evidently I dozed off.

Suddenly, in my sleep or daydream I heard the crackle of a breaking branch behind me. I could see nothing through the darkness, when suddenly a burst of automatic fire flashed from the dark woods. I bent low over the steering wheel, put the jeep into gear, and accelerated away in the direction of the command post. My left wheels were on the right edge of the road; my right wheels were rolling through the forest edge, crushing little shrubs and saplings. Several more bursts of gunfire rang out. The Germans were firing down the length of the road, or, more properly, the forest track, because it was visible against the backdrop of the night sky. As I was driving to the right of the road, the bullets passed me harmlessly.

I drove to the command post and reported what had happened to the officer on duty. He sounded the alarm, and all the special units were summoned to action. Under the command of the scout platoon leader, they quickly set off for the place of my close escape.

In the battalion area, where they were handing out the medals, they also heard the bursts of automatic fire and rushed to rescue me. The battalion's relief force arrived prior to the special units. The major knew where I had parked the Willys, and surrounded that spot with several groups. Crossfire erupted; the encirclement tightened and netted seventeen German prisoners. At the interrogation, the commanding German *obergefreiter* [the equivalent of the rank of corporal in the American armies] said that his group had the task of sneaking through to our regimental command post, destroying it, and taking some prisoners—hopefully, even the regimental commander himself. But on the way, they caught sight of my car's headlights and were forced to stop. The German raid had been neutralized and the command post saved from attack. The regimental commander thanked me for the timely warning of danger.

The Sudden Death of a Comrade

After nearly a week with the 9th Guards Airborne Regiment, I began to feel comfortable. I had become acquainted with everyone, and I had made visits to several sections of our defensive lines.

A local success on the left flank of the regiment had allowed it 47
to improve its positions and to capture several German "trophies"
[captured equipment]. There were vehicles among the trophies. Senior Lieutenant Kozak decided to have a look at them and, if possible, to adapt them to the regiment's use.

Three of us set out for the location of the vehicles: Guards Senior Lieutenant Kozak, Slava, and I. We safely managed to reach
the place where the vehicles were standing. They were parked in a
little field among some small pine trees about three to four meters
high. I began to examine a Steyr, while Slava and Kozak looked over
an Opel Blitz truck. I carefully circled the Steyr, checking for mines.
I found nothing suspicious, neither did I when I peered through
the window and examined the driver's seat and steering wheel, nor
when I crawled inside.

Finally convinced the car was safe, I began to study its condition.
It had a half tank of fuel and a normal level of oil. The battery was
fully charged. I started the motor and it worked cleanly. I put the
car into gear and tried to move, but nothing happened. I came to
the conclusion that the transmission coupling with the engine was
broken. It was going to be necessary to tow the vehicle back to the
regiment's rear area. We tried to tow the Steyr with the Willys, but
had no luck: the Steyr was heavier, and we could not manage to
haul it through the sandy soil back to the road. The heavy Steyr
kept bogging down. Evidently, this is what had caused the Germans
to abandon the vehicle in the first place. It had bogged down in the
sand, and given that our Russian soldiers were approaching quickly,
the German driver had broken the transmission coupling and fled,
leaving the key in the ignition.

We couldn't start the Opel Blitz truck, but it seemed otherwise to
be in good condition. Senior Lieutenant Kozak decided to return to
the command post and request permission to take the ZIS-5 truck,
still loaded with military supplies, and use it to tow both German
vehicles back to the command post. The regimental commander
agreed to this proposition only reluctantly. We set out again on a
second trip to the trophy vehicles, this time in two vehicles, the Willys and the ZIS-5.

We approached their location, about five kilometers away, safely.
I was leading in the Willys, while Ivanov followed in the ZIS-5.

While we had traveled to the command post, the situation at the front had become more complicated: the Germans were trying to regain their former positions and were counterattacking.[1] German fighter-bombers were supporting the infantry attack. At the very moment when our trucks had reached within 200 meters of the trophy German vehicles, five Me-109 fighter-bombers began to dive upon us. I managed to turn my Willys off the road to the left and to hide it under some trees. The ZIS-5 remained on the road, with Ivanov inside it.

Concealing the Willys beneath the branches of trees, we three—Kozak, Slava, and I—abandoned it and took cover wherever we could find it. As we abandoned the car, the first bombs released by the Messerschmidts were exploding, and I was showered with leaves and little branches. I had run about fifteen meters away when a bomb's shock wave knocked me to the ground. I didn't notice where Slava and Kozak had run. They had jumped from the Willys sooner than me, as soon as I began to slow it to a stop. I didn't leave until the jeep had stopped fully, about three seconds later.

The German pilots had spotted our vehicles and bombed accurately, especially since Ivanov had not managed to hide the ZIS-5 in the woods and left it standing on the open road. The German planes made two passes. After the bombing run, they returned to strafe the area with machine guns.

After the fighter-bombers left, I got up and examined the Willys. It was not badly damaged—just a few holes in the body and right splashboard. Then I walked over to the ZIS. It was in worse shape: the front windshield and headlights were smashed, the radiator had been punctured and had leaked out its fluid, and the cabin door had been half torn away. I found Ivanov in a pothole in the road about thirty meters from the truck, and about forty meters from a bomb crater. Ivanov had been wounded in the right arm and right leg. Fortunately, the wounds were not severe. I dressed his wounds, then helped him to the Willys and placed him on the front seat. I shouted for the others. No one answered.

I began to look around for the others. About twenty-five meters from the trees, beneath which I had parked the Willys, I spotted Slava lying facedown. I called to him, but he didn't respond. I walked up to him and looked him over. At first, I didn't notice any wounds. I carefully turned him over onto his back, and discovered that he had been completely disemboweled. He had no pulse, and wasn't breathing. Slava was dead.

I collected his documents from the pocket of his tunic. I covered his body with a piece of tarpaulin I found in the back of the ZIS, and set off in search of Senior Lieutenant Kozak. Judging by everything, I had suffered less than everyone else. I had been knocked down by the shock wave of the first bomb explosion. Luckily, I had been knocked to the ground behind a small mound, about fifty centimeters high, at the foot of some small trees. The slight rise had protected me from the fragments and shock waves from the bombs. I escaped with bruises to my arms and legs, and a ringing in my ears from a light concussion.

I also examined the Steyr and Opel Blitz. A bomb had landed between them and turned them into heaps of twisted metal.

I could not find Senior Lieutenant Kozak anywhere nearby. I decided to return to the command post with the wounded Ivanov to report on what had happened. I hoped to encounter the senior lieutenant along the road on the way back. We drove slowly, carefully looking around us and shouting his name, occasionally giving audible signals with a Klaxon. During the time I had spent tending to the wounded Ivanov, Sasha's body, and inspecting our ruined German trophies, Kozak could not have walked farther than one and a half kilometers. Having traveled that far with no sign of him, I drove faster.

At the command post, I reported on what had happened and asked for soldiers to return with me to the ZIS, to guard the vehicle and to help me retrieve Slava's body. They gave me two soldiers, and we left together. We reached the spot just before twilight. Along the way I gave the soldiers instructions what to do in case the Germans managed to push back our front lines and approach the ZIS. In this case, unless they were able to repel the enemy, they were to wet a padded jacket with gasoline and set fire to the ZIS.

We found the ZIS, and the two comrades helped me put Slava's body in the back of the Willys. I left them guarding the damaged truck, and I set out in return to the command post by the most direct route. Having traveled about two kilometers from the place of Slava's death, I spotted Senior Lieutenant Kozak, with a bandaged head, sitting on a stump to the left of the road. I picked him up and took him with me. We hadn't traveled another one and a half kilometers back to the command post when the Willys' engine seized up. Senior Lieutenant Kozak left on foot for the command post, while I remained with Slava's body.

It was night. Silence reigned. I checked the motor again. Yes, it was frozen up. It made no sense to disassemble the vehicle here, since I had no replacement connecting rod bearings with me. In Willys trucks, in distinction from our own trucks, the main and connecting rod bearings were not overlaid with Babbitt metal. Instead, they were made from steel bushings, the working surface of which was covered by a layer of an elastic but durable alloy. The thickness of the layer was such that it would last for 20,000 to 30,000 kilometers.

Through lend-lease the United States supplied us with many small, simple, and inexpensive jeeps like the Willys. The Willys jeeps were used primarily as personal transport for commanders of the Red Army. In addition, the trucks towed 45-mm and 76-mm anti-tank guns. They had decent speed, excellent off-road capability, and were quite powerful. The vehicle had a supplementary gearbox, which allowed the operator to reduce the speed and increase the towing power. It had both front- and rear-drive axles.

The compact size, simplicity of operation, maneuverability, and inexpensiveness of these vehicles gave the jeeps a long life and high popularity among us in the Red Army. Even decades after the war, in film sequences from foreign documentaries I could see these "hard workers" at the service of the American army.

The United States magnanimously gave us these vehicles and spare parts for them. The American leaders knew that without spare parts, the vehicles would eventually wear out and no longer be useful. However, for some reason the spare parts never seemed to reach the combat units; probably they were being concentrated at repair facilities far in the rear. I had personally gathered a small supply of these bushings, which were calculated for a guaranteed period of use by the vehicle. However, near Ponyri I had lost them during one of the artillery bombardments, and I was forced to fashion them from empty 45-mm shell casings.

I laid Slava's body on the backseat of the Willys and covered it with half of a tent. I lay down on the front seat and wrapped myself up in the other half of the tent. But before I lay down to sleep, I loaded a PPSh submachine gun and laid it by my head—just in case. Around the truck's gearshift I placed two F-1 hand grenades. I also took my TT pistol from its holster and laid it by my jacket. With some difficulty I got comfortable on the front seat and fell asleep.

I woke to the twitter of birds. Otherwise it was quiet. I got up and stretched. I glanced at Slava's body. An unpleasant odor was beginning to emit from it. We were taking it to the command post, in order to bury it there in the regiment's fraternal cemetery, which had already begun to grow. However, the situation had developed that I would be forced to bury him here, if a tow didn't appear in the next hour or two.

Waiting for a tow, I began to investigate the surroundings, in order to find a place where I could bury Slava. Not far from the truck's position, I found several small ditches, which could be adapted as graves. A little farther on, I came upon gun pits of the regiment's howitzers, and nearby, a stack of shells. Walking around the ammunition pile, I found a soldier lying in one of the emplacements. I listened closely: he was breathing, alive. . . . I woke him up. He stood up. It turned out that we were both from the 9th Guards Airborne Regiment. His battery had changed firing positions. It had advanced closer to the front lines and had left him behind to guard the ammunition. About one and a half hours later, I asked the artillerist to help me carry Slava's body to one of the little trenches and bury him.

Before we laid Slava to rest, I took the boots from his feet and laid them in the back of the Willys. We buried Slava in the deepest pit, but its depth was only eighty-five centimeters. We didn't have a shovel, so we were forced to dig the grave with a helmet and the empty casing of a 120-mm shell. Once we had made the grave mound, next to it we planted a little birch tree, about one meter tall.

The artillerist who had helped me was wearing *botinki* [peasant-style low boots] with puttees. I offered Slava's combat boots to him, but he declined, having sworn from the very start of the war to wear nothing but ankle-high boots. The artillerist was older than me by about twenty years and had obviously joined our airborne division as a replacement somewhere before the crossing of the Dnepr, since "pure" airborne troopers were between eighteen and thirty years of age.

Toward the end of the day, a tow finally arrived for the Willys and me—a pair of heavyweight artillery horses. Back at the command post, we remembered our fallen comrade Slava. Guards Senior Lieutenant Kozak took it upon himself to send Viacheslav's personal documents to his wife. At that time, she was also serving on the front in the Leningrad area.

At the Repair Station

It was impossible to repair the Willys in field conditions, so it was necessary to take it to the location of the division's transportation battalion. It was situated on the bank of the Dnepr in the village of Domantovo, where we had recently made our forced crossing. I had to wait three days, until my jeep was towed to that place.

Domantovo was a typical steppe village. In addition to the rear elements of our division, the 18th Guards Rifle Corps' headquarters and the army's evacuation hospital were located here. While I worked on repairing the Willys, I found accommodations in a little shed belonging to a peasant, not far from the transportation battalion's parking lot. I stayed in the shed, because the peasant's hut itself was full of wounded. During the day, I worked on the jeep; in the evenings I helped a nurse, Tania from Kineshma, take care of the wounded. There were approximately twenty-five severely wounded men in the hut, with only one nurse to look after them. I helped Tania re-dress and bandage their wounds, and in the morning and evening I would bring two buckets of food from the hospital kitchen and feed all those who wanted to eat but were incapable of sitting up. In the evenings, I also made cigarettes for the patients and passed them around to give them a chance to smoke. I helped them to the toilet, as many of the men felt embarrassed to go in front of Tania. I spent two weeks in this village, while the basic repair on the jeep remained unfinished, since it was impossible to find bushings for the connecting rod bearings anywhere. Since the Willys was the only one in the 9th Guards Airborne Regiment, it was impossible to borrow spare parts for it from within the regiment.

My Second Wounding and Another Transfer

I returned to the regiment's command post and resumed my chauffer duties. On 3 November 1943, I was traveling with the regimental commander somewhere far from the front lines. Along the way we spotted another broken-down German vehicle. I asked permission to stop and check out the vehicle's condition, to see if we could use it. I got out of the Willys and began walking toward the abandoned vehicle. As I walked, a bullet flew out of nowhere and struck me in a fleshy part of my upper leg. The bullet buried itself there, and they sent me to the hospital.

As soon as I recovered, I was sent to the 65th Army in the First Belorussian Front. A reserve regiment there was preparing an expedition to requisition foodstuffs for the army, and the purchaser had been looking for drivers. I was taken to 65th Army headquarters, where the special unit was preparing to depart on the food-gathering expedition to Chernigov Oblast. The officer in charge of the expedition, Lieutenant Colonel Sychev, had a Willys and needed a chauffeur for it. I wound up with him.

For several months, I acted as a driver while the unit gathered agricultural produce for the 65th Army in ten districts of Chernigov Oblast. In each district there was a designated collection point, to which the collective farms and state farms brought their produce: wheat, flour, corn, groats, beef, chickens, vegetable oil, and butter, all in the quantity designated for them by the district authorities. Times were very difficult for the people in these regions because the land had been devastated by war and the Fascist "scorched-earth" policy of retreat. But the army did not have to seize food from the peasants—Soviet authority engaged in this. We never encountered any resistance from the civilians in the area, firstly because Soviet power excluded this possibility; secondly because the local population at that moment consisted of old men, women, and children; and finally because the obligations of food produce for the army were placed on collective farms and state farms, not individual households. There were bandit "nationalist" groups operating in the Ukraine at this time, but not in Chernigov Oblast. These anti-Soviet groups were operating farther to the west. I acted as Lieutenant Colonel Sychev's driver until April 1944, at which time my military service took a sudden turn in an unexpected direction.

Chapter 5

Operation Bagration

During the late spring of 1944, the Red Army was preparing for its summer offensive. This included the First Belorussian Front and the 65th Army. All officers and men were part of this training and preparation, including the 91st Transportation Battalion to which I had been posted. We were ferrying supplies to units and supply dumps in the immediate rear areas of the army. At that time, a commission arrived to inspect the operations of our transportation battalion. They found certain shortcomings in its work, and the battalion's commander, Avdonin, was removed and reassigned to other duties.

My Violation of Duty and Punishment

Before his departure, Avdonin invited a cook, several signalmen, and me to accompany him to his new position. He told us, "I have received a new assignment, and I'll take you with me." He left for his new position in the 18th Auto Transport Brigade. From there he sent his personal driver, Litvin Zotov, back to us with a letter. It was not an order, but a personal letter from Avdonin as a battalion officer to come join him. The signalmen were sensible and refused the invitation, but the cook and I, suffering a momentary lapse of reason, dashed off to join Avdonin. We arrived, and he assigned us to his own personal detail within the battalion.

Within two weeks, an investigator, a SMERSH captain, arrived and summoned us to battalion headquarters. There he informed us, "I have orders for your arrest and to take you back to the 91st Transportation Battalion under escort. Although you did not voluntarily abandon your unit, you left in response to a letter, not an order. Therefore, you are considered deserters."

They took us back to the battalion, and the new captain, Ratnikov, sentenced us to three months in a penal company—the 261st Separate Army Penal Company. This company consisted of soldiers, sergeants, and officers who had committed disciplinary infractions or criminal offenses. Among the latter in our company was the crew of an IL-2 "Shturmovik." In a fit of jealous rage, the pilot had mown down his squadron commander, whom he suspected of paying excessive attention to his wife. Remaining members of our company had been sent here for desertion, tardiness in returning from leave, or for pillaging.

In my experience, discipline in the penal company was only a little stricter than in the average rifle unit. Rather than taking roll once a day, as was usual, they checked twice a day. The commanders of the company also had to constantly supervise the subordinate men in the company. Otherwise, there was little difference between the daily life of a soldier in this penal company and in a regular rifle company. Our food rations were the same, as were our weapons and the amount of combat supply we received. So where was our punishment? Penal units were always sent to the most dangerous sections of the front, to the enemy's most fortified places. Once there, they were expected to conduct reconnaissance forays, take prisoners, and then lead the assault when an offensive began. But it is curious to note that after serious military engagements, the surviving members of penal companies received three to five days of rest and recreation, while the men who served in regular rifle units continued combat operations, regardless of their losses.

Before Operation Bagration, they combined my penal company with other penal companies to create a special penal assault battalion: two companies of submachine gunners of up to 100 men each, a separate machine-gun platoon, and another small support platoon of submachine gunners. There were altogether 273 men in this special assault battalion.

I wound up in the machine-gun platoon. Our battalion commander, Vinogradov (a fine man!), came to our dugout one evening and said, "Fellows, help us out: we need to create a platoon of medium and heavy machine gunners." There were thirteen of us in the dugout—all chauffeurs—and we all agreed to volunteer. For about two weeks, we trained on the machine guns. We became familiar with their operation, learned to disassemble and reassemble them, and learned how to control their fire. When they formed four machine gun teams, I was given command of one of them. Our team consisted of eight men, and the weapon I commanded was a Model 1910 Maxim heavy machine gun. This gun was water-cooled, fired a 250-round belt of 7.62-mm bullets at a rate of 520 to 580 rounds per minute, and was the Red Army's basic heavy machine gun during the war.

56   They gave us our combat equipment and supplies. The Number One in the team carried the gun barrel; the Number Two carried the gun carriage; the Number Three carried the gun mount, shield, and a cartridge belt; while the remaining members of the team carried up to two cartridge belts each.

Operation Bagration Begins

By the spring of 1944, the strategic initiative had long since passed into Allied hands. On the Eastern Front, a series of sledgehammer blows in the previous winter had broken the German siege of Leningrad in the north; in the south, the victorious Red Armies had largely cleared the Ukraine of Axis forces. Now as planning began for the summer offensive, the attention of Stalin and the Stavka turned to Belorussia, where the German Army Group Center occupied a prominent, fortified bulge in the lines north of the Pripiat' River, in the Vitebsk-Orsha-Mogilev-Bobruisk area. Hitler declared each of these cities "fortified regions," and as was his predilection, the German salient encompassed a precarious bridgehead beyond the Berezina River.

The "Belorussian Balcony," as the Germans referred to Army Group Center's position, was vulnerable to encirclement and destruction. Hitler believed that Army Group Center's front was static and would not be seriously tested in the summer of 1944. Accordingly, he had mistakenly transferred nearly all the panzer divisions on the Eastern Front southward to the Ukraine below the Pripiat' River, where he believed the main summer Soviet offensive would fall. The defenses of Army Group Center had little depth, as most of its defending forces were deployed in the first line of defenses. The Stavka accordingly believed that conditions were favorable for delivering deep, concentric blows against Army Group Center in the general direction of Minsk. If successful, it would lead to the encirclement and destruction of the preponderant force of Army Group Center, which was defending fixed lines well to the east of Minsk.

The Stavka's operational plans envisioned the main attacks on both flanks of the German "Balcony." In the north, First Baltic Front and Third Belorussian Front would combine to destroy the misnamed Third Panzer Army (which actually had no panzer divisions at all) defending the Vitebsk-Orsha region, and move upon Minsk from the north. In the south, First Belorussian Front would defeat the Ninth Army's defenses around Bobruisk and then move upon Minsk from the south. In the center, Second Belorussian Front would launch strong holding attacks against the strongest section of

Army Group Center's defenses in the Orsha-Mogilev region, defended by the Fourth Army. If successful, the plan envisioned the entrapment of the Fourth Army, plus large numbers of the Third Panzer and Ninth Armies.[1]

Using extensive security and deception measures, during the month of May 1944, the attacking Soviet armies steadily marshaled a marked superiority over the enemy along the entire Belorussian front.[2] But Soviet operational art preferred strongly to concentrate dense numbers of men, tanks, and field guns at designated breakthrough sectors, and at these places, the Soviet numerical advantage grew to overwhelming proportions. For example, along the First Belorussian's entire sector of the front (approximately 240 kilometers long), the Soviet forces built up a 2:1 superiority over the defending Ninth Army in combat personnel, a 3:1 advantage in field guns (76-mm and up), and an 8:1 advantage in tanks and self-propelled guns. However, in the fifteen-kilometer breakthrough front south of Parichi, the First Belorussian Front's superiority over the Germans grew to nearly 6:1 in combat personnel, 22:1 in field guns (76-mm and up), and 16:1 in tanks and self-propelled guns.[3]

Before the offensive, Soviet intelligence and reconnaissance had established that in the Bobruisk sector, the defending Ninth Army (consisting of the III and LV Army Corps and the XXXXI Panzer Corps) had up to twelve infantry divisions in its first line of defense, and only four security divisions and one panzer division in its operational reserve. Ninth Army had established its densest defenses and concentrated its forces on the Rogachev-Bobruisk axis. Following Hitler's command, Bobruisk itself was turned into a fortified city and center of resistance. The Ninth Army's commander evidently considered the marshy terrain south of this axis as unsuitable for attacking forces. Hence, the defensive positions south of Parichi were inadequately fortified and often consisted of a single trench covering open areas for firing. Rokossovskii's plan of attack exploited this shortcoming in the Ninth Army's defenses. He intended for the 3rd and 48th Armies to break through German defenses north of Rogachev, while the 65th Army and the 1st Guards "Don" Tank Corps would sweep north through Parichi, sever all enemy lines of communication approaching Bobruisk from the west, then cooperate with the 3rd and 48th Armies in the capture of Bobruisk.

The southern axis of Rokossovskii's planned attack would have to pass through the northern fringes of the great Pripiat' Swamp. It remained for General Batov to find some way for his forces, and the tanks of the 1st Guards "Don" Tank Corps, to negotiate the swampy, wooded lowlands on the approach to Bobruisk from the south.

On 22 June 1944, the great summer offensive designed to crush the enemy's Army Group Center began. It was called Operation Bagration, after the famous Russian general of the Napoleonic era, Pyotr Bagration (1765–1812). We were located in Kalinkovskii District, near Ozarichi in Belorussia, under the command of the 354th Rifle Division.

For several weeks prior to the beginning of our offensive, the commander of the 65th Army, Colonel General P. I. Batov, had been searching for the best point of attack for his army. Traveling together with an army engineer, the head of army intelligence, and others, they toured the sector of the advance allotted to the 65th Army. The German defenses here were strong, as there were good roads in the area, and much of it was suitable for tank movement.

While examining a swampy section of the line to the left of Parichi, they spotted some of the army's scouts, who were wearing woven "swamp shoes." They were made from broomcorn stalks, and worn over the boots. These swamp shoes reduced the ground pressure of the soldier's step, and as the soldier stepped, the peat beneath his foot would condense and not bog him down. Water would percolate up through the gaps in the weave, and as he raised his foot for the next step, the water would then drain away through the woven footgear. One Belorussian soldier who lived in the area showed General Batov how hunters used this footgear to get through the swamps. Batov thought a while and then decided to conduct the main point of his attack here, where the Germans least expected it. In addition, from this point, Red Army tanks could cut the road between Parichi and Bobruisk within thirty minutes (see map 3).

To enable passage of the tanks and other heavy equipment through the swamp, Batov ordered a wooden plank road to be constructed. The logs for the planking were cut and prepared 15 to 20 kilometers from the front, so the Germans would not hear the noise of the felling of trees and the sawing. The planks were prepared and joined by cramp iron into sections. These were brought up to the front to within about 200 meters of the crossing and camouflaged. In this way, the plank road could quickly be laid after the leading infantry had already crossed the swamp and created a "bridgehead" on the other side.

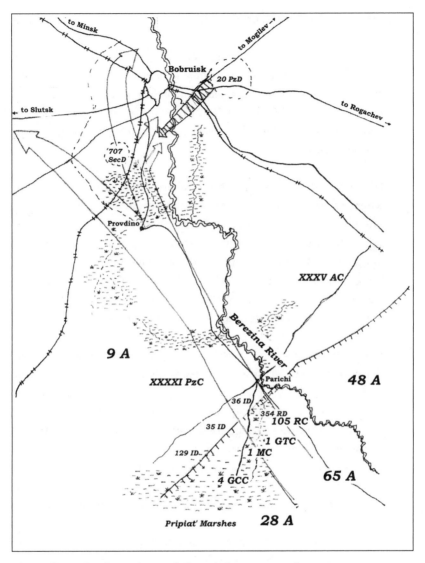

Map 3. Operation Bagration, 65th Army's Sector, 24–27 June 1944

We Lead the Attack on Parichi

The town of Parichi was an important objective on the way to Bobruisk. Several roads converge on Parichi from the north, west, east, and south, making the town an important local road hub in the generally marshy terrain of the area. The German XXXXI Panzer Corps' 36th Infantry Division screened Parichi, but Litvin's testimony indicates the weakness of German defenses in this area.

For our small part, we in the special assault battalion didn't know where we were going. On 22 June, the order came to move out. We didn't know that our advance was merely a demonstration, designed to distract the Germans' attention from the main blow of our assault. We simply marched for two days, our assault battalion leading the way for the rest of the 354th Division.[4] In the distance, we could hear the sounds of battle. Our machine-gun jackets were not filled with water, in order to make it easier to march. The machine gun used up to three liters of water to cool the barrel during firing. Our orders were to follow the road from Kalinkovichi, and the next morning cross a little stream (its name I now forget) and capture Parichi.

The ground was rather swampy, as our division was marching through the northern fringes of the great Pripiat' Marshes—terrain almost impassable to armies. I was feeling very upset and angry as we marched because I had received word that morning from my mother that my younger brother Alexander had been killed in battle at Vitebsk. He had been called up to serve in a reserve regiment in Petropavlovsk two months after my departure for active duty. At the beginning of 1942, Alexander wound up at the front with the 473rd Rifle Regiment of the 15th Rifle Division, where he served as section commander. In the battles northeast of Vitebsk near the village of Miskhi, he had died in action on 25 December 1943.

We had reached a hillock somewhere just short of Parichi and stopped to rest among some previously prepared trenches, when suddenly from the other side of a small stream a Ferdinand opened fire on us. Its first shell fell short of our trenches and exploded on the slope below us. We quickly took cover in the entrenchments, all 273 of us. The Ferdinand raised its sights a little and fired again, but this time the shell flew harmlessly over us. The Ferdinand fired fifteen rounds and never once hit the target. Evidently it had exhausted its ammunition, as it turned around and drove away.

After the Ferdinand left, we cautiously began to emerge from the trenches. A German heavy machine gun at the edge of some woods across the stream, alerted by the sound of the Ferdinand's shelling, caught sight of the flashes from our helmets. It opened fire on us. The first burst sent us dropping back into the trenches, and fortunately no one was hit. A second burst flew overhead. Our platoon commander gave the order: "Litvin, silence that machine gun!"

I chose an elevated, covered piece of ground on which to position our machine gun, and some of our team set the weapon up while others ferried water to us from the reverse slope so we could fill the cooling jacket before opening fire. I told my second, "Sania, today I myself will shoot the gun and avenge the death of my brother." When the German machine gun opened up again, I gave it a long burst (fifteen to twenty rounds) from my Maxim, and then two short bursts (five to six rounds each). The German machine gun immediately fell silent. Some comrades raised a helmet on a stick above the trench line, and the German machine gun didn't react. Evidently, I had knocked out the machine gun position.

After a couple of minutes of silence, we received the orders to move out and cross the stream. Nearby, our battalion advance found a ditch running down the hill to the stream. Since it provided some cover, they picked their way down and found a ford. They waved back at us, and I began to take down my machine gun, and then we began to move toward their position.

Suddenly, we could hear the sound of mortar rounds flying through the air. Evidently, some German officer had received notice that a large group of Russian infantry was approaching and had decided to dispatch vehicles mounting 81-mm mortars to the threatened location. We hadn't noticed their approach, and only when they opened fire did we catch sight of them. To our great fortune, next to the ford in some bushes were four large pits, which had evidently been excavated at some time during the war in order to conceal vehicles. They were about four meters wide, nine meters long, and two meters deep. As soon as we heard the mortar rounds falling, the men of our battalion dove into these pits for cover, tumbling into layers of men desperate for shelter. I could feel someone landing atop me, and I was lying upon some other comrade. The first mortar shells erupted around us, and the Germans fired no less than ten shells per barrel during the barrage. They laid down their shells in a genuine sheaf of fire.

The German mortar barrage cut down every shrub in the fire zone to the ground, and they were confident that not a single Soviet soldier remained from our battalion. They gathered up their mortars and drove back to Parichi. However, not a single shell had landed in any of the pits, and all had exploded around us harmlessly. We crawled out of the pits, covered with earth and debris, and many of us had light bruises from the collision of bodies as we dove into the pits. We crossed the stream at the ford, and on the other side discovered a heap of heavy machine-gun cartridge cases, and some blood traces on the tall grass. The German machine gun had been positioned here.

By now it was growing dark, and we could see that the Germans were situated in a belt of woods, where small lights were twinkling. But they were no longer shooting at us. My machine gun was ordered to support a submachine gun platoon, and we began to discuss plans for approaching Parichi in the morning. Next to the road leading to the belt of woods and Parichi beyond, I found a sumptuous clump of hazelnut, and I placed my machine gun here. From this position I planned to conduct covering fire while the platoon of *avtomatchiki* advanced upon the Germans occupying the belt of woods.

However, when we began our attack the next morning, the Germans were no longer in the positions they had been occupying the night before. We cautiously moved on toward Parichi and found the Germans falling back on the road between Kalinkovichi and Parichi. The road here cut through a rye field and meadow, which contained a large burial mound.

The Germans engaged us and undertook a fighting withdrawal toward Parichi. Our *avtomatchiki* fired as they advanced. We trailed behind, looking for places from which we could cover the attack of our infantry with our machine guns. As the Germans reached the outskirts of Parichi, they took cover, and their resistance stiffened. Our advance slowed, and soon we were engaged in a heavy exchange of fire. After about three hours since we had moved out that morning, the ammunition for our submachine guns began to run out, and the fire from our *avtomatchiki* dwindled.

The Germans noticed this weakening of fire and immediately counterattacked, wanting to drive us back from Parichi. They moved out from their cover, firing as they advanced. The sharp German counterattack caught us by surprise, and we fell back in some disarray about 200 meters. My comrades in the machine-gun platoon abandoned three of our machine guns but removed their locks and brought away the ammunition. (The Germans later found the weapons and blew them up with grenades.) I looked for a place to set up my machine gun and placed it on the large burial mound in the meadow.

When the German counterattack erupted, we could hear the sound of German tanks starting up in Parichi, and a mortar battery emerged on the outskirts of the town and deployed. With my single remaining machine gun, I opened fire at the targets about 600 meters away. I saw one or two of the Germans fall, but of course the majority remained alive and set up their mortars for firing.

The first German mortar shell exploded about thirty meters behind our position, while the second shell landed about twenty meters in front of us. They had our position bracketed, so I gave the command to the machine-gun crew to move the gun to the left. We made the move safely, because of the shelter of the large burial mound where our machine gun had been standing. Within a few seconds of our departure, the burial mound behind us disappeared in a black cloud of explosions and smoke from the German mortar barrage. One of my team was lightly wounded, but we all managed to escape and to hide in some tall grass.

At this point, the 1199th Regiment of the 354th Rifle Division reached the battlefield, bringing up fresh ammunition. The battle intensified. "Katiusha" rockets roared overhead toward the Germans.[5] I fired from our new position until we had exhausted our ammunition, at which point the other members of my team began running away. Yes, I was left alone with the machine gun as my comrades on the team fled. This was not a violation of discipline, but simply common sense. They had exhausted the ammunition in their personal weapons, and with no more ammunition for their submachine guns, they left. Unfortunately, they took with them the cartridge belts for the machine gun, and someone had grabbed my own submachine gun as he retreated. I was left with the empty machine gun, while they had all the ammunition for it.

A bullet whistled over my head, and I understood that the Germans had me in their sights. I lay low in the tall grass and tied one end of a field belt to the machine gun, the other end to my leg. I began crawling away, dragging the machine gun behind me as I sought to escape the aim of the German that had spotted me. I don't know how far I had managed to crawl, perhaps just five or six meters, when I raised my head and saw a Russian soldier walking toward me, carrying a rifle. He was from the 1199th Regiment. Suddenly another bullet flew closely past me. The Russian soldier spotted the German who had fired the shot, and killed him with a return shot. He calmly blew into the barrel of his gun, then asked me: "Are there any other Germans who want some?" I later learned his name was Turchin.

I asked him to help me drag the machine gun to a new position, and he agreed. Once we reached it, Turchin walked on. I spotted a member of my machine-gun team and called for him. Somehow the Germans spotted me again, and they lobbed some mortar rounds in my direction. I threw myself into a nearby foxhole. The explosions practically buried me in a torrent of cascading dirt. Only my head and part of one arm remained above ground, and I couldn't breathe or move a muscle.

At that moment, two lads in green military caps from the so-called blocking detachments walked up to me.[6] One calmly asked, "What's this?" I told them, "Fellows, help me out." They dug me out, and then asked, "Why are you sitting here? Advance!" I replied, "Advance with what? I have only an empty machine gun. I have none of my comrades or my ammunition. When they come, we will advance." This was the only time during the war that I saw one of these blocking detachment soldiers alive. But in actuality, these two were border guards. Border guards were often called upon to serve in these blocking detachments.

Our battalion commander received the order to withdraw from the battle, as the 1199th Regiment of the 354th Rifle Division had continued the fight for the village and had taken it. By this time, I had joined eleven of my comrades from the penal battalion, including five machine gunners from my crew and six submachine gunners from the support platoon of *avtomatchiki*. We were together when a messenger arrived and gave us the order to fall back to a field kitchen that had been set up in a hollow not far from Parichi. While we headed back to the kitchen, more of my gun crew formed up with us. When we first reached the kitchen, I feared our battalion had taken heavy losses, as many men were missing. We grabbed a quick meal at the kitchen, and then left a machine gun and two men to help guard the kitchen, while the rest of us went back into Parichi to look over the situation.

As we approached Parichi, we spotted a weak blood trail. We followed it, and in the German entrenchments we came upon a German who seemed dead. We went to rummage through his pockets to look for documents. But the German was alive, and before we reached him, he jumped to his knees and shouted in Russian: "Russian, don't shoot!" Turchin ordered, "Get your hands up." The German replied, "My hands are already up." He turned out to be a Slovak. We took him with us and turned him in at the prisoner collection point. The Slovak wasn't a bad guy. Although he had to hold up his pants with his hand so they wouldn't fall after Turchin took his belt from him, he smiled all the time.

In Parichi we found a cellar that had some wine. We grabbed it, returned to our camp, and discovered that while we were gone, much of the penal assault battalion had assembled at the field kitchen, along with the rest of my gun crew. I shared the wine we had found with the rest of the crew, and we all hoped for a good night's sleep. But that very evening, the order came to move out for Bobruisk.

Slaughter at Bobruisk

Our battalion set off with the rest of the 354th Rifle Division for Bobruisk, while other elements of the 65th Army, with accompanying armor from the 1st Guards "Don" Tank Corps, crossed the swamp behind us. Meanwhile, a cavalry mechanized group headed for the city of Slutsk, to the west of Bobruisk.

Steadily, we plodded on toward Bobruisk. Everyone was walking without his full combat kit, and we were pulling the machine gun along. I suddenly noticed: the gun shield was missing. "Vasen'ka, where's the shield?" I asked. He had tossed it aside, to lighten his load and make his march easier. I told him, "I know nothing, but that shield had better reappear by the next halt."

After walking about twelve kilometers in the direction of Bobruisk, the battalion came to a halt and placed three lookouts by the road to direct straggling members of our battalion to our location. At this halt, approximately 30 more members of the assault battalion, who had been left behind in Parichi, arrived in fine style, riding self-propelled guns. They brought with them a fifty-liter cask of wine. With their addition, our battalion now had about 200 men. At further halts in our march, we encountered more men from our penal battalion, so our losses at Parichi were not as large as I had first feared.

On the following day—28 June—we received the order to halt our march and dig into a defensive position. Germans constantly harassed our position with tracer rounds, but nobody on our side was hit. We positioned our machine gun next to a shed. That night, we sent out our scouts to locate the German positions opposite us and to knock out the machine guns that were pestering us. They managed to destroy several German positions and found two machine guns.

The next morning, we waited for the assault on Bobruisk to begin at 10:00 A.M. While we were waiting, a little dog ran up to our position. It looked like a jackal, and it kept running back and forth until we followed it. The dog led us to a dugout that was filled with water. When we peered inside, we spotted motion in the water. A sergeant fired a burst from his PPSh, and then we heard someone cry out, "Rus, don't shoot!" From out of the dugout crawled eight soggy Slovak soldiers. They had been given the order to blow up an 81-mm mortar, so that it wouldn't fall into our possession. Instead of following their orders, they had hidden in the dugout. We sent them on to the prisoner collection point.

Later, we moved out under scattered harassing fire. As we advanced, Belorussians emerged from cellars, some offering intelligence on the Germans. Little boys seemed to know everything about the Germans—where they were and what they were doing. They led our column to the northwest of Bobruisk, to a cemetery. Along the way, we gathered up many abandoned German weapons and much equipment. We also found a lot of liquor. I warned my machine-gun crew members not to drink. It seemed that the Germans had deliberately left a lot of liquor for us to find as we advanced, so that the Russians would get drunk and they could seize us with their bare hands.

Yes, some Russians got drunk, but not all. I remember well one episode from that day involving a comrade who could not resist the temptations of the liquor. As we marched toward Bobruisk from the west, we paused in our advance near a church that overlooked a town square and a large cemetery. The cemetery was thickly overgrown with shrubs. An immobilized German tank was in the square, not far from a wall surrounding the church.

I selected a position for our Maxim machine gun behind the church wall. The position had a superb field of fire toward the cemetery, as the entire square lay out before our sights like the spread palm of an open hand. While the gun crew set up the machine gun, I strolled over to inspect the abandoned German tank. Its machine guns were still in place, and I noticed that there was ample ammunition inside the tank.

I headed back to my gun crew. Just as I reached them, gunfire erupted. It was about 2:00 P.M. As we had anticipated, the Germans were trying to launch a counterattack through the cemetery. Taking notice of the hostile gun positions in the cemetery, I ordered my gunner to suppress them. Leaving him to this task, I crawled forward to the knocked-out German tank, which stood about fifty meters from the churchyard wall in the direction of the cemetery. I managed to reach the tank and crawl inside. Once there, I felt like a fish in water. I loaded a machine gun and began to fire it at all enemy positions I could see, and I raked the edge of the cemetery with sweeping fire.

When the crossfire began, many of our infantry were nearby, not yet in position. They quickly rushed to deploy and became engaged in the battle. About ten minutes after the firing began, a horse-drawn cart emerged from around a side of the church, carrying three soldiers. One whipped the horses, while the other two fired a machine gun from the cart. The cart moved across the large square toward the cemetery for about 80 meters, then stopped and turned around. The machine gun fired several bursts at the enemy, and then again the cart began rolling forward.

From the other side of the church, a drunken *avtomatchik* rode out upon an unsaddled horse. In his right hand he held his PPSh submachine gun with its characteristic round cartridge disk, and in his left hand was a bottle of beer. He encouraged the horse to move by pounding on its back with his fist. Occasionally, he let loose a wild burst from his submachine gun, then immediately followed it with a swig from the bottle.

The Germans evidently saw that it would be suicide to try and cross the empty square, so they settled into an exchange of fire that lasted about thirty minutes. At that point, under the cover of fire from our two machine guns, our infantry and submachine gunners rushed the cemetery and scattered or destroyed the Germans who had held it.

By 5:00 P.M. on 29 June 1944, our battalion reached the northwest suburbs of the city of Bobruisk along the Minsk highway. The 354th Rifle Division together with our assault battalion stopped and dug into a defensive position not far from the highway, facing to the east. The Germans defending Bobruisk were now caught in a noose.

Two kilometers from our positions to the east were two small villages. Inside them were the remnants of surrounded hostile forces that had not yet been destroyed. We expected that under the cover of darkness, these Germans would make an attempt to break through to the west, across the Minsk highway and into the woods beyond.

From our positions, a thin belt of woods separated us from a large rye field that stretched to the two villages. We placed our machine gun on a small hillock on the edge of the woods overlooking the highway, so that in case of necessity, we could sweep the highway with fire in either direction, toward Minsk or toward Bobruisk. In front of our position, a gap in the woods about thirty-five meters wide gave us a clean field of fire toward the rye field, across which the Germans would be advancing.

We emplaced our machine guns, marked a few reference points for aiming, and then sat down to rest. It was about 6:00 P.M., after a long, hot day. I took off my boots. I had worn them continuously for more than a week. I wiped my feet with alcohol from a pocket flask in order to cool them off. It was twilight, and we had a quick supper.

Suddenly, we could hear bullets whipping past us in the trees. The Germans were firing explosive bullets, which were striking the tree branches above us and exploding. The gunfire intensified. Everyone grabbed their weapons and checked their ammunition supply. Near my machine-gun position there were many of our supply carts with their drivers. Most of these drivers were older than fifty years, and they had never before experienced combat. A panic began among them. They began to saddle and harness their horses to flee. We turned our machine gun upon them and I shouted, "Stop, don't move!" Younger soldiers approached them and told them, "Lay down, grab your weapons, and together we'll drive the Germans back!" They obeyed.

Suddenly a large column of Germans moved from the village toward the Minsk highway, perhaps 10,000 strong. They were marching in column, as if on a parade ground. The column was 100 to 120 meters wide, and perhaps no less than a kilometer long. It was heading to our left. There were two vehicles in the middle of the column, each one mounting American Oerlikon guns.[7] Most likely, these guns had previously been ours, but we had let them slip into German hands. The guns were pouring fire into our positions. The column apparently planned to break through our lines here, cross the Minsk highway, and pass through the woods we were occupying.

As it approached the highway, the column deployed into a human wave and rushed forward. From our position, the left flank of the German line of advancing men was about 1,200 meters away.

We opened fire on the Germans, not permitting them to turn in our direction. The Germans were packed so tightly together, and in such a mass, that it was simply impossible to miss. When our command found out that a German column was attempting to break out here, they rushed an antitank battery to our support. Twelve cannons unlimbered before the column and began to fire at it over open sights. They fired fragmentation shells first, and then when the German avalanche had approached within range, switched to case shot. Once they had expended all their case shot, the guns switched to whatever they had remaining, even armor-piercing rounds. The fighting was desperate and continued until nightfall. Having lost perhaps half their force, most Germans fell back to the village. Perhaps 1,500 Germans managed to break through our lines and escape. On the field of battle remained piles of German corpses and the seriously wounded.

In the morning, we woke up and looked out upon the field of carnage. It was quiet. There was no shooting. The rye field was a mousy color from all the fallen Germans in their field gray uniforms. Their corpses lay piled upon one another. It was another hot day. Our machine gun remained pointed toward the village to where the remnants of the trapped German force had retreated. By 11:00 A.M., a stench began rising into the air.

By the middle of the day, my comrade Alexander ("Sashka") Shulepov and I decided to walk into the village to investigate. Soviet troops had already entered the village and were rounding up prisoners. I left my gunner in charge of the machine gun, and Sashka and I made sure we were carrying full disks of ammunition for our submachine guns.

Germans soldiers were sitting everywhere, looking at us in complete resignation. There were no officers. Perhaps they had already been rounded up, or else they had fallen on the field of battle the day before. The Germans knew they were trapped, and they were simply waiting for our troops to gather them up. They watched us out of the corners of their eyes as we passed. They were afraid we would shoot them.

We walked along the main village street perhaps 400 meters, when suddenly we heard a piercing wail and loud lamentations from a nearby household. We headed over to investigate and found an old woman crying over the corpse of her husband. A younger woman told us that one or two Germans had stopped by their place the day before, demanding eggs and milk. The residents didn't have any, so the Germans had executed the grandfather on the spot. At this moment, a column of German prisoners was passing by the house. The grieving woman recognized one of the culprits among the prisoners. The old woman and her neighbors rushed to the prisoner convoy and told the guards what he had done. The German was a tall, thin man. We asked the convoy guard to turn this prisoner over to the women. The guards resisted at first, but after persistent entreaties, handed him over. The women rushed upon the prisoner and, in their fury, literally tore him to pieces with their bare hands.

We began to head back to our position in the woods and overtook another column of German prisoners. There was a sturdy, healthy young man walking in the column, who was plainly not German. Sashka asked him, "Are you a Russian?" He answered in fluent Russian, "Yes, from Krasnoiarsk." He had been captured by the Germans in the first months of the war and had managed to survive prison camp. A German officer had come to the camp one day to recruit for Vlasov's Army.[8] This Russian had volunteered in the hope of one day escaping somehow, after he had regained his strength. But he had come to like being among the Germans and had never tried to run away. He never served on the front lines, but in antipartisan units in the rear areas. He said they had been well fed and clothed. He told us, "Three years passed like three days."

He said he didn't regret his service in the German army, or feel sorry for our burdens in the Red Army. We couldn't stand listening to this and asked the prisoner convoy guards to hand over this "fellow countryman" to us. They yielded him to us and marched on. We led the prisoner to the side of the road. He said, "I know you are going to shoot me, but I'm not going to beg you to spare me. If I was in your place, I would shoot you right away." Shulepov couldn't take such talk, and shot the Russian traitor once in the chest and stomach. The prisoner didn't even flinch, but just made a wry face and asked, "Is that really how you shoot? Well, give me another round." Sashka fired a burst of at least twelve rounds across his chest and into his head. The traitor fell. Of course, Sashka could have been punished for this violation of discipline, but where could they send him? He was already in a penal battalion.

Afterward, I was tormented by these cruel and gory scenes of violence and struggled to regain my composure. It was a strange matter. During the fighting for Parichi, I had felt a different sensation. I was striving so that each one of my shots might find a body to strike, so that I could kill as many of the enemy as I possibly could, because they had come to kill my brother, and now they were after me. But now, after the death before my eyes of two unarmed enemies, I was in a different state of mind and had different feelings, even though these opponents had deserved their fate. Yes, the judgment over two unarmed people had been arbitrary, but these people themselves had started the vileness—and we had finished it, so as to finish it forever.

On 1 July, we remained in our positions in the woods overlooking the Minsk highway. We took turns watching over the machine guns in pairs. In the middle of the day, the battalion commander ordered all officers to prepare commendations for all the actions from Parichi to Bobruisk. The commander of our platoon, a lieutenant, selected me and one other fellow to fill out the forms. We were given the last names of the honored soldiers and a short summary of their deeds. All this we had to put down onto the forms. I was ordered to prepare a commendation for myself. I submitted my name for the Order of the Red Star, for saving my machine gun during the fighting before Parichi, and for personally destroying an enemy machine gun detachment during the German counterattack through the cemetery on the road to Bobruisk. About twenty soldiers from our penal battalion received honors. On 3 July 1944, in the very same position on the road between Bobruisk and Minsk, the battalion commander announced that I would receive no commendation, that instead I would receive an immediate discharge from the penal battalion. They freed Shulepov along with me. Thus ended my career as the commander of a machine-gun team, as a member of a penal battalion, and my service in a rifle unit.

Shulepov and I were assigned to the 354th "Kalinkovichi" Red Banner Rifle Division. Our comrades in the penal battalion remained where they were. I turned my machine-gun team over to my gunner, and said farewell to my comrades. We had atoned for our guilt before the Motherland, the law, and our comrades in arms.

The author, Nikolai Litvin, and Svetlana Nizhevskaia pose at Litvin's work desk.

The author, Nikolai Litvin, in his mining industry uniform, Ol'chansk, 1952 (author's personal collection)

Officers and men of the 6th Separate Guards Airborne Tank Destroyer Battalion, during a brief pause in preparations for the defense of the Kursk bulge. First row, right: Tumarbekov; second row, right: Commissar Kleshchev, holding a cigarette. Over Kleshchev's left shoulder, battery commander Captain Bondarev, who helped dig Litvin out of his premature grave during the battle (author's personal collection)

A confident Colonel
V. N. Dzhandzhgava,
commander of the 354th
Rifle Division, during
Operation Bagration, July
or August 1944 (author's
personal collection)

V. N. Dzhandzhgava (left)
and his deputy political
commander, V. K. Butsol,
1945 (author's personal
collection)

General P. I. Batov, commander of the 65th Army, postwar photograph (author's personal collection)

General D. F. Alekseev, commander of the 105th Rifle Corps, 1973 (author's personal collection)

Officers and troops of the 105th Rifle Corps, posing by the walls of the Reichstag, May 1945. General D. F. Alekseev (left) and General V. N. Dzhandzhgava are flanking the woman in the front row (author's personal collection)

Colonel V. I. Piatenko, commander of the 1199th Rifle Regiment, 354th Rifle Division, wartime photograph (author's personal collection)

Litvin crouches behind a 45-mm gun in his gunlayer's position, forty years after the battle of Kursk, 1983 (author's personal collection)

The 2005 ceremony at the unveiling of a monument at the grave site of Hero of the Soviet Union Guards Lieutenant G. F. Bastrakhov, who fell in battle near here, while fighting to foil the German relief effort to free German divisions trapped near Cherkassy, January 1944. Litvin is standing in his light blue paratrooper's beret, third from left (author's personal collection)

In 2002, Litvin poses by the grave site of his younger brother, who was killed in action near Vitebsk, 25 December 1943 (author's personal collection)

Chapter 6

Into Poland with the 354th Rifle Division

Long after the war, General Batov, commander of the 65th Army, recalled the manner of the pell-mell advance to the old national border after the capture of Bobruisk. He wrote: "The special feature of the offensive in this period was the wide use of mobile detachments. Each division detached one or two rifle battalions, strengthened with several tanks and self-propelled guns. The tempo of the advance reached up to thirty to forty kilometers a day. Moving along parallel rural roads in vehicles, the detachments advanced far ahead of our main forces, cut the enemy's probable routes of retreat, and met him with unexpected fire."[1] Since Litvin was moving with the headquarters, not with one of the mobile detachments or even a main body rifle unit, he was not witness to the action at the tip of the division's spearhead. However, he provides another interesting perspective on this advance and was not isolated from the horrors of war.

Two chauffeurs, two Siberians, two former punished soldiers arrived at the command post of the 354th Rifle Division before evening of the very same day, 3 July 1944. The divisional command post was situated just 300 meters or so from "Shurochka," our penal battalion.

Upon arrival at the 354th Division, we were assigned to the headquarters' platoon. We comprised the chauffeurs' reserve for the divisional headquarters. The headquarters' platoon commander received us. He was small, and like a toy lieutenant, curtly acquainted us with the facts of the matter. He informed us that we would not be assigned to formal posts, but that he would give us assignments as he saw fit. We would be moving with the divisional headquarters, and since we were chauffeurs without cars, we had to consent to traveling on foot.

On the next day, early in the morning we moved out on foot in the direction of Baranovichi. Along the road we were traveling, troops were moving in long, dusty columns. It was warm, but we had no water or food. We marched the entire day. Tanks and artillery must have been moving in front of us, because we saw only supply wagons and large groups of infantry. The movement proceeded without any attempt to camouflage or disguise it. Enemy aviation did not bother us, and we encountered no enemy ground forces. We marched forty kilometers that day, and we were designated to march sixty kilometers the next day.

An Unwanted Duty

The next morning, however, the divisional commander asked that Sashka and I take six prisoners back to corps headquarters. It was located eighteen kilometers away on the route we had just taken. Before we left, we were told that we could deal with the prisoners at our own discretion, if we grew tired of escorting them. I understood this to mean that the prisoners were marked for execution, and I was to be an executioner.

None of the six prisoners was a regular officer; they were all mobilized reservists of various ages. Among them was one young man, about seventeen years of age, tall and thin. He looked very much like a garden scarecrow, since he was wearing a dress coat too large for his thin frame. The other men were much older and had families at home.

Our little prisoner column moved slowly, as the elderly men among them could not walk quickly. It seemed we were all tired and hungry. Sashka twice proposed that we execute them, but I was opposed to this idea. But Sashka continued to remind me of our commander's hint to dispose of the prisoners quickly. I did not want to shoot the prisoners, but I felt the weight of command. I also knew that the successful advance had netted tens of thousands of German prisoners, overwhelming the prisoner collection stations. Six more prisoners were worthless, especially in this brutal war.

At some point, Sashka stopped the prisoners and moved them off the road. It was plain that the prisoners understood Sashka's intentions and they didn't take their eyes off his submachine gun. They showed us their calloused hands. They had been metal workers before the war. Some looked us in the eye and cried for mercy. I felt very sorry for them, as my own father was a metal worker, and he had also been called to war, and he also wanted to return home safely to his family. I was in a state of emotional turmoil, especially after witnessing the killing of the two unarmed prisoners previously. Sashka kept reminding me of my duty. We raised our submachine guns. Sashka fired first, and the youngest German dropped to the ground, writhing in agony. All the horrors of war that I had witnessed welled up inside all at once, and as I squeezed my trigger, I fainted. When I regained consciousness, I could see all the prisoners lying dead on the ground, and Sashka waiting for me by the path we had taken. I checked my submachine gun and found it was missing several rounds, and suddenly I realized what had happened.[2]

For days afterward, as we marched along, I was tormented by what I had seen in Bobruisk, and what Sashka and I had done to the prisoners. I had signed up to fight a war, and killing an armed opponent in battle did not trouble me. But the mass slaughter of the Germans trying to break out of our ring at Bobruisk, the summary execution of the Russian traitor, the savage revenge killing of the German prisoner taken from the prisoner column, and the execution of these reservists had filled my mind with terrible images of execution and death, and I was sickened by this war.

For the return to the 354th Rifle Division's command post, we climbed into a truck that was carrying supplies to the division. Along the way back, I conversed with a fellow in the truck, a gypsy with the last name Ganzha.

When we returned to the command post, I caught sight of a colorful figure with a little mustache like Charlie Chaplin's. Everyone was bustling around him. It was Colonel Vladimir Nikolaevich Dzhandzhgava, who had recently assumed command of the division from Dmitri Fedorovich Alekseev. Alekseev had been promoted to command the 105th Rifle Corps prior to Operation Bagration. Colonel Dzhandzhgava had previously commanded the 15th "Sivash" Rifle Division.

Transferred Again

We hastened our advance to Baranovichi, and beyond to Slonim and Bialystok, by using all possible means and types of transportation. Many soldiers attached supply wagons and peasant carts to tanks and self-propelled guns, and then hopped in for the tow. Many others traveled in carts being pulled by confiscated horses, ox, and even goats. We passed Baranovichi quickly and traveled through Slonim in the middle of the day. The city was empty. The citizens remained inside their homes and hid. Since we had to hurry on to Bialystok,

I didn't see any major violations of discipline in Slonim. Sashka and I spent approximately a week with the headquarters' platoon, and then we were transferred to the 473rd Separate Transportation Battalion of the 354th Rifle Division.

Captain Afana'ev, the commander of the battalion, and his adjutant Senior Lieutenant Gorshkov were interested in our experience. Sashka had worked previously on pickup trucks, but I had worked only on Willys jeeps. This was great! The transportation battalion had a worn-out Willys that no one could repair. They handed it over to me for my care. I started on the repair work, and within two days I managed to get the vehicle "back on its feet" and became its designated driver. This was excellent; after all, to drive around is better than walking around! The repaired Willys and I were placed at the disposal of the deputy divisional commander, Lieutenant Colonel Davydkin. After a week of trips with Lieutenant Colonel Davydkin, I knew all the units of the division.

By this time, the war had reached the old national border. One day, before departure from the command post, Davydkin announced that we would be heading to a large manor in the great Bialowiecz Forest. We arrived there around noon. The manor was heavily damaged. We found Colonel Dzhandzhgava there, and many other officers. There I also saw for the first time our 65th Army commander, Lieutenant General Pavel Ivanovich Batov. The weather was bright and sunny, but the enemy's air force made no visits. Batov ordered us to disperse into the nearest woods, just in case of an air raid.

We crossed the Polish border in the district of Biabzhega. Rumors traveled among the troops that this was the birthplace of our *front* commander Rokossovskii. Troops pointed out a farmstead where his parents lived.

Immediately upon crossing the Polish border, I noticed a change in the landscape. Farms were neatly arranged, and the soil was carefully tilled. You could sense the spirit of individualism. Among the peasants here, everything was "my," while in the Soviet Union, everything was "our" in the kolkhozes. We asked the peasants, "Why aren't you together, in a collective?" And their answer? "My." For the first few days, the local Polish people looked at the Soviets and communists as if they had horns on their head, and at us, Siberians, as if we liked to devour little children.

Kleshcheli and Avgustinka

On 28 June 1944, Hitler relieved Field Marshal Busch of command of German Army Group Center and appointed Field Marshal Model in his place. Model took over command of the shattered remnants of Army Group Center while simultaneously maintaining command over the bordering Army Group North Ukraine to the south. Model's task was to try and patch together a new line of defense to mend the 450-kilometer-wide gap that Operation Bagration had torn into the German line. This unusual command arrangement allowed Model to shift reserves of Army Group North Ukraine to Army Group Center, and Hitler granted permission for this to Model. However, at this time of the war, the Germans simply did not have enough divisions and transportation to meet the demands of the situation, and Model was never fully able to fill all the gaps in Army Group Center's line. By this time of the war, the Soviet command had become highly adept at identifying weak points and gaps in the German defenses and had sufficient mobility to exploit these opportunities.

By mid-July, one such gap appeared in the Bialowiecz Forest, a densely forested, partisan-rich region northeast of Brest-Litovsk. Unfortunately for Model, only a small Hungarian mobile unit was lightly screening this forest, and it lay on the boundary between the German XXIII Corps, which was trying simultaneously to hold open the collapsing Pinsk pocket and withdraw from it, and Corps Harteneck, which was trying to shield Bialystok to the north. It only took a little pressure for the Red Army to rip apart contact between the two corps on 13 July. The First Belorussian Front commander, Rokossovskii, sent the 65th Army crashing into this gap along a high-capacity road that ran through the Polish villages of Kleshcheli and Siemiatycze to the Western Bug River. Once across this river, the 65th Army would sever the German XXIII Corps' supply lines and pose a direct threat to Brest-Litovsk from the north. This threat prompted a vigorous German reaction, which Litvin describes below.[3]

Despite expectations, we passed through the Bialowiecz Forest relatively easily and quickly. Once through the forest and onto the more open terrain beyond, the pace of our advance was high, and our special forward mobile detachments overcame the enemy's resistance. Leading elements of the 65th Army reached the Western Bug River and established several small bridgeheads beyond it near Siemiatycze (see map 4).

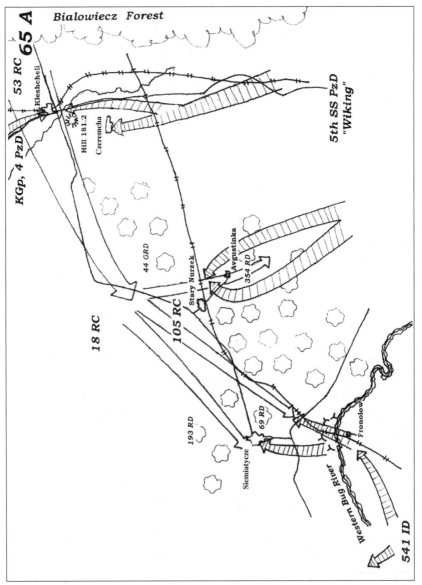

Map 4. Kleshcheli–Avgustinka–Western Bug Operations, 19–25 July 1944

The spearheads of our army dug in hastily while they awaited the arrival of our main forces. However, our army's advance had surpassed those of our neighboring armies to our right and left, the 28th and 46th Armies, by thirty to forty kilometers and left behind exposed flanks. The German command, having discovered the 65th Army's vulnerable position, decided to surround it and destroy it.

The 65th Army's penetration was long and narrow as it squeezed between the German XXIII Corps to the south and Corps Harteneck to the north along the high-capacity road to Siemiatycze. Model saw an opportunity to cut off and eliminate the 65th Army by launching a pincer attack at the salient's neck at Kleshcheli. The XXIII Corps' 5th SS Panzer Division "Wiking" struck at Kleshcheli and Avgustinka, a village lying on the road to Siemiatycze about halfway from Kleshcheli, from the south. Kampfgruppe Christern of Corps Harteneck's 4th Panzer Division attacked toward Kleshcheli from the north, trying to link up with a kampfgruppe from 5th SS Panzer Division's "Westland" Regiment. Finally, XX Corps' 541st Infantry Division attacked the tip of the narrow Russian penetration, with orders to eliminate the shallow bridgeheads that the 65th Army had created across the Western Bug River.

In the area of the village of Kleshcheli, the enemy, with tanks, tried to cut off and surround the forces of the 65th Army that were plunging forward to breach the Western Bug River. Enemy tank forces did manage to link up but were unable to seal firmly the penetration of the 65th Army. A narrow passage—only about a kilometer wide—remained along the road forward from Kleshcheli to Avgustinka and the Western Bug River beyond. The German counterattack forced the 65th Army to withdraw its lead units from across the Western Bug River and to conduct strong attacks from the east and west to try and reopen a secure line of supply. Elements of the 65th Army, including the 354th Rifle Division, took up a circular defensive position in the area of Avgustinka, and waited for resupply.

The battle quickly became confusing. By the time of the German counterattack on Kleshcheli, neither the Soviet 65th Army's elements in Avgustinka and beyond nor the German SS "Wiking" Panzer Division had a secure line of supply. Supply became an important factor in the outcome of the struggle.

On the eve of the German counterattack, the deputy divisional commander visited the divisional commander. Colonel Dzhand-zhgava's command post was situated in a church in the village of Avgustinka. Units of the division were located about six to eight kilometers west and south of Avgustinka, seeking to link up with the 4th Guards Cavalry Corps, which had broken through German lines farther to the south and east. Under the initial blows of the German counterstrike, these divisional units had to retreat and oc-cupied a circular defense in some woods, ten to twelve kilometers west of Kleshcheli. By the middle of the next day, 23 July, it had become clear that encircled elements of our division were putting up stubborn resistance to the attacking German forces. The deputy divisional commander received an order to lead personally a supply column to Avgustinka with ammunition and food. The commander of the transportation battalion received an order to prepare some loaded trucks, while I was told to prepare my Willys.

For several days now, the Willys had been running poorly. Some-where air was getting sucked into the fuel system, and thus the engine was not getting enough fuel for normal, uninterrupted op-eration. I hadn't been able to locate the problem, so therefore I had to drive in short intervals of three to five kilometers, then stop and blow through the fuel system with a pump. The pumped air would create some additional pressure on the fuel, and the engine would run smoothly for the next seven to ten minutes. After just three to five kilometers, I would have to stop and repeat the whole process. I was afraid that the engine would cut out along a section of the road to Avgustinka that the Germans had taken under fire. Just in case, I attached a light towline to the front bumper of my jeep, so that one of the trucks could tow me if my engine cut out.

After loading the trucks, our supply column moved out and ap-proached Kleshcheli from the east. We stopped in the middle of the village, so that the deputy divisional commander Davydkin could check out the road ahead. While we waited, I persuaded all the other drivers to keep a watch out for my signal for help, in case they started overtaking me.

Davydkin moved up to the western outskirts of Kleshcheli, where our tanks and infantry were exchanging fire with enemy positions overlooking the road. Enemy troops were occupying a hill to the left of the road from Kleshcheli to Avgustinka,[4] and from this position they were shooting at our troops in Kleshcheli and sweeping the road to Avgustinka with fire.

Taking cover behind one of our T-34 tanks standing by the side of the road that exited the western side of the village, we were able to determine that enemy infantry had taken position approximately 200 meters from the road down which our supply column had to travel. Enemy mortars were conducting sporadic fire. Given the urgency of our mission, Lieutenant Colonel Davydkin decided to send the entire column at once through the fire-swept section of the road at top speed. While the deputy divisional commander was arranging covering fire for our venture from the tanks stationed on the edge of Kleshcheli, I managed to pump a considerable amount of air into the fuel tank of my Willys in order to put the fuel supply system under pressure. We would have to travel about four kilometers while exposed to enemy fire.

Lieutenant Colonel Davydkin climbed into my Willys, and we set off. All the drivers were ordered to drive faster than normal and in a compact column, but when we began to receive intensive fire, they were to disperse, but keep moving forward. From the edge of Kleshcheli to the enemy-held hill, at the foot of which ran our road, the entire column passed safely. The tanks had opened heavy harassing fire on the enemy's positions and kept the enemy infantry pressed to the earth. My vehicle ran at the head of the column. The column was moving under the deputy divisional commander's order to "do whatever I do."

Once we reached the foot of the heights, the column of trucks was safe from small arms and machine gun fire, but soon we began to receive mortar fire. However, the mortars were firing indirectly from covered positions on the reverse slope of the hill, so they couldn't see the results of their fire or easily correct their aim and range. The road was level, and I was driving as fast as I could. I sped ahead of the column of following trucks by about 600 meters, tore through the fire zone, and stopped. We looked back at the column of trucks to see what was happening. Heavily loaded, they moved more slowly than we did, but without any sign of panic. Thus our supply column broke through to our surrounded comrades in Avgustinka at 6:00 P.M., 23 July 1944, with the loss of only one truck.

Rolf Hinze's history of this campaign asserts that the 4th Panzer Kampfgruppe did manage to seize Kleshcheli in the late afternoon of 23

July and established a most tenuous connection with the 1st Battalion of the 5th SS Panzer Regiment, but that lack of supply forced both divisions to abandon their positions in the Kleshcheli area and withdraw to their departure areas. This brief linkup must have occurred after Davydkin and the supply column left Kleshcheli for Avgustinka.

Once we reached our destination, the trucks set out to deliver supplies to all the various units in the pocket, while the deputy divisional commander headed for the divisional command post in my Willys. The command post was situated in a church on a small hill to the southwest of the village. Coniferous forest surrounded the church, and the woods were full of our troops.

From Kleshcheli to Avgustinka my vehicle ran smoothly. While Lieutenant Colonel Davydkin conferred with Colonel Dzhandzhgava in the church, I parked my car about 80 meters away by the side of a road that led down a slope into the forest. The forest was about 150 meters away. After about five minutes, while I waited for the deputy divisional commander, I heard the engine hum of approaching airplanes. I looked up—Junkers! They were heading straight for the church. I leaped out of my Willys and shouted, "Air raid!" Then I gave the jeep a push and hopped into it as it was rolling, and without starting up the engine, coasted down into the forest where some tanks were parked. As I reached the tank park in the woods, bombs had already begun exploding around the church. I dove beneath the nearest tank for cover. The bombing raid ended, and I crawled out from beneath the tank. I ran up to the church, and found that no bombs had struck it. We spent the night there, as all the supply trucks in the column remained with the units they had supplied.

Heavy fighting continued for three more days, as the 65th Army sought to secure its line of supply. Corps Harteneck quickly had to disengage from its attempt to link up with SS Panzer Division "Wiking," as powerful attacks by the Soviet 48th Army threatened to swamp it. SS Panzer Division "Wiking" attempted to hold a position around Czeremcha, a key railroad town just four kilometers south of the Soviet 65th Army's supply route along the key Kleshcheli-Avgustinka road. From hills just to the north of Czeremcha, "Wiking" could keep the supply route under observation and threaten Soviet supply convoys. From 24 to 26 July, the 65th Army kept the hills and town under heavy artillery fire and launched repeated heavy in-

fantry attacks on "Wiking's" positions. Eventually, "Wiking" had to aban-
don this position and withdraw back across the Western Bug.

On the morning of 24 July, we resumed our efforts to secure our supply line. Eventually, we smashed out of the pocket and advanced forward. The 65th Army had lost seventy-two hours in the Kleshcheli-Avgustinka cauldron.[5]

About a week later, as we were driving to the city of Vyshkov for one of Lieutenant Colonel Davydkov's regular meetings with Colonel Dzhandzhgava, we came under fire. A spent shell splinter penetrated the bridge of my nose and became stuck there. I could see it with my eyes. A second splinter buried itself in my neck. My neck swelled up and I couldn't turn it. Lieutenant Colonel Davyd-kin ordered me to drive to a medical station. When we got there, Davydkin told the doctors and nurses, "Ladies, take a look at my beauty. He sits there as stiff as a poker, and turns his head like a wolf." They laid me down on a table, gave me some anesthetics, and waited for me to fall asleep. But I didn't fall asleep. Doctor O. L. Baryshnykova told me, "What, do you drink a lot of vodka?" I replied, "No." And she asked, "Then why aren't you falling asleep?" They gave me another dose of anesthetics, and only then did I fall asleep. I had a dream. It was as if I was still a machine-gun team leader, and my crew was returning from a reconnaissance foray with a prisoner from Vlasov's Army. In my dream, it turned out that the prisoner was the brother of Masha, a nurse who was Lieutenant Colonel Davydkin's girlfriend at that time. My comrades were ask-ing me what to do with him, and in my dream, but out loud, I told them, "Shoot him!" When I came to after the surgery, the nurses were laughing: "Did you shoot someone there?" They had sewn up my wounds, and quickly it became easier for me to turn my head.

A few days later, during a regular visit to the divisional com-mander, it became known that his driver for the GAZ-57 had been wounded. They took the wounded driver to a field station, then to a hospital in the rear, but they left me "at the front"—at the forward battle zone. Colonel Dzhandzhgava's adjutant explained that I had to stay here until they could find a suitable replacement driver.

Once along the road to the divisional commander, my engine died and I was stuck along the road for a while—about twenty min-utes. Upon my arrival at headquarters, the chief of staff was very curious about the reason for my delay and about where I had been stuck. His curiosity was not incidental—in this area, there were cases where some of our officers and soldiers had disappeared without a trace. Polish nationalist partisans were operating in the area, and there were occasional sorties by small groups of Germans.

During my first trip with Colonel Dzhandzhgava, he asked me about my parents and my past. Most likely, he was the one who had written the order that released me from the penal battalion in exchange for the Order of the Red Star.

The Narev Bridgehead

The Narev River flows through the northeastern part of Poland. It begins in the Bialowiecz Forest in Belorussia and flows southward in an arc for more than 400 kilometers before it enters the Vistula River north of Warsaw.

After we had fended off the German counterattacks in the area of Avgustinka and Kleshcheli, we had crossed the Western Bug River and continued our westward advance at a somewhat slower pace. Operation Bagration had worn out the Germans, but it had worn us out too. We continually pursued the enemy, while they continued to frustrate our advance with covering detachments and local counterattacks.

Front commander Rokossovskii became concerned that his *front* was falling behind in the race to Germany, so he gave orders to General Batov of the 65th Army to seize a bridgehead across the Narev River no later than the first week of September. Rokossovskii designated an area between Pultusk and Serotsk, north of Warsaw, as the location of our bridgehead, and it had to be large enough to prepare a major offensive into the depth of German territory from it.

The divisions of the 65th Army were in a weakened state by this time. We had advanced more than 600 kilometers since the beginning of Operation Bagration, and in the ensuing two and a half months of advance we had lost more than half our personnel in the ceaseless fighting.

However, on the morning of 5 September 1944, tanks from the 1st Guards "Don" Tank Corps forced a crossing of the Narev River. On the eve before, tanks had tried to take a bridge over the river off the march. But the Germans had mined the bridge, and they blew up both ends of the bridge as our tanks approached, even though the bridge was full of retreating Germans. Those Germans who were lucky enough to remain standing on the intact middle section of the bridge jumped into the river and tried to swim to the western shore. This stretch of the river contained no other bridges or fords, and for our forces to cross it now required considerable ingenuity and courage.

At this point, the Narev was a rather serious obstacle to our advance. It was up to 200 meters wide and flowed at a depth of up to six meters. The 1st Guards "Don" Tank Corps came up and received the order to cross the river underwater. By this time, it had few operational tanks left; only eighteen or so remained to undertake the crossing.

I watched as the tank crews caulked up every slit and crevice on their tank and installed tall pipes to supply air for the engines and to vent the exhaust. Once this work was finished, the crews connected the tanks with steel cable, one after the other, just in case an engine flooded and a tank required a tow. With that done, the lead tank slid into the water, and the others followed one by one. They success-fully reached the other side and immediately moved to guard the crossing while many infantry paddled across on makeshift rafts.

Behind the tanks and the advanced infantry, artillery began mov-ing to cross. The gun crews undressed and drove their horses across the river, dragging their guns behind.

As the units crossed, they moved out to expand the bridgehead. In the first few hours, it was only one and a half kilometers deep. Sappers were busy constructing a wooden bridge in the vicinity of Vul'k-Zatorsk. When it was finished, the remainder of the 65th Army began crossing. By the evening of 5 September, more than half our infantry were across the river.

The Germans reacted to this development in their typical style and tried to drive us out of our bridgehead. For four days fighting seethed. We fought to expand the bridgehead, while the Germans tried to eliminate it. Ultimately, the Germans failed to reduce the bridgehead. The regiments of our division managed to get astride the road between Pultusk and Serotsk, advanced approximately eight kilometers, and then dug into fortified positions. It was im-possible to expand the bridgehead any farther, since we didn't have sufficient strength. Although our bridgehead across the Narev was shallow (in the sector of the 354th Rifle Division, it was less than eight kilometers deep), Rokossovskii considered it very important and demanded that General Batov stubbornly defend it.

After the failure of the initial German attempt to drive the 65th Army back across the Narev, a pause in the fighting occurred. We sought to reinforce the bridgehead as much as possible, while presumably the Germans regrouped and brought up reinforcements of their own. But the rate of replacements we received was a trickle. Instead of the 6,000 men we needed to return to full strength, we only received 800. Among them were some Moldavians, and we learned about the liberation of Moldavia from them.

During this lull, I was serving as the chauffeur for the deputy divisional commander in charge of the division's rear services. The rear of our division was located in a pine forest along the left (east) bank of the river, between the settlement Vul'k-Zatorsk and the river itself. The wooden bridge was about a kilometer away. In the mature pine forest, all the rear elements and services of the 354th Rifle Division were located. The ammunition stockpiles, the 473rd Transportation Battalion, the division's medical field station, and other elements were situated on the extreme southwest edge of the forest. The village of Vul'k-Zatorsk itself accommodated the division's headquarters, SMERSH, the procurator, and the military tribunal.

The personnel of the transportation battalion and the personnel of the medical field station lived in dugouts. Wounded men had the shelter of hospital tents. There was also a log bathhouse with steam. After long weeks of hard marches and battles, our accommodations seemed almost luxurious.

My Willys jeep was running as well as it could—which was not very well. The engine was taking its last breaths; therefore, we decided to replace it with the engine from a captured "Citroen." The installation was a difficult matter in field conditions for the following reasons: (1) The point of fastening the clutch housing to the gearshift box was different. (2) We had to shorten the primary shaft of the gearbox, and we faced other similar alterations.

Fitting the replacement engine into the Willys took more than two weeks. At last I reassembled the vehicle, started up the engine, and the Willys started off. I was moving, and gathered speed. I successfully shifted from first gear into second. I put it into third gear, and my vehicle began moving backward. It turned out that when I took apart the gearbox to take out and shorten the primary shaft, I mixed up the gears and thus had two speeds—forward and reverse. I was forced to take out the gearbox for the third time and switch around the gears—but without result. I worked on the Willys for another week, and it was only after I found a gearbox in a captured German light vehicle similar in layout to that in the Willys did I fix the problem.

From time to time since the start of my service, I had received letters from home from my mother, and from my father in active duty elsewhere in the Red Army. During our pause in the Narev bridgehead, the mail caught up with us again and I received new letters. My mother was working at a factory that produced *makhorki,* the crude, cheap cigarettes that were popular in those difficult years. I learned my fifteen-year-old brother, Leonid, was working at a small engine factory. My seventeen-year-old brother, Anatolii, was working at a naval ammunition factory. From my father's letters, it became clear that he was in the Crimea, and his division was taking part in the forced expulsion of Tatars from the Crimea, but it was also engaged in preparations for the Yalta conference of Allied powers.

After the engine was replaced, the Willys was working tolerably well. On one of the first days after completing the repair, I drove up to the deputy divisional commander's quarters and encountered a familiar officer. It was Major Georgii Chirkin. Previously, in 1943–1944, he was serving as a captain as a technical assistant to the commander of the 91st Army Transportation Battalion, where I first became acquainted with him. After receiving his promotion, Chirkin was recalled from the 91st Transportation Battalion and assigned to head the auto services of our division. We greeted each other like family members. The major expressed a wish to resume our joint service together, but the head of auto services was not supposed to have any assistants of any kind, so he was unable to get me reassigned to him. As we parted, he promised me an assignment as one of the division's motorcyclists.

Meanwhile, I remained in my post as chauffeur for Lieutenant Colonel Davydkin. Around the middle of September, we received a batch of new replacements for the transportation battalion. They were young fellows, all born in 1926, who had completed a course of training as chauffeurs. But we had no need for chauffeurs, so instead they were left to do small repairs on broken-down vehicles, general camp duties, and guard duty. Among them there was a certain Kiselov, with whom fate eventually drew me much closer together.

94   The Counterattack on the Narev

The successful offensive of our troops from Parichi and Bobruisk allowed us through battle to push back the enemy lines 600 kilometers in a little more than two months. By this time, we had pressed the enemy beyond the borders of the Soviet Union. The Germans viewed our bridgehead on the Narev River as a pistol, pointed at the heart of Germany.

At 6:00 A.M. on the morning of 5 October 1944, I heard the thunder of an artillery bombardment. It reminded me of the sound I heard when the heavy guns began firing near Ponyri, but here I was eight kilometers from the front line, yet the sound of battle was clearly audible. I happened to be standing guard by a stockpile of combustible lubricants at the time. The German attack was a complete surprise and seemed to be focused on the Dzerzhenin sector of the front (see map 5).[6]

The commander of the training battalion of our division, Captain Grechukha, a good friend of mine, later described the battles for the bridgehead:

No one talked of any possibility of a German counterattack then. Everyone was confident that the enemy no longer had the forces or means for an attack. According to our scouts, the Germans had constructed a dense, multilayered defense surrounding our bridgehead, with many permanent fieldworks and minefields. In the tactical and nearest operational depth of the enemy, intelligence had not noticed any significant combat groups. Only a few intelligence officers had pricked up their ears at the evidence from radio interceptions that our radio technicians had picked up at the end of September. A particular German radio station had twice issued a coded message about the readiness to go over on the offensive. The intercepted messages did not indicate the direction of the forthcoming blow. The heightened state of readiness among our troops that this intelligence prompted passed away when no attack followed. It seemed that these transmissions were just another German trick.

The night of 4 October seemed no different from any of the preceding nights. There were sporadic bursts of machine gun fire, and the occasional round of artillery, to which we had become accustomed, seemed to presage no threat. As usual, at dawn they began delivering hot breakfasts from the field kitchens to the trenches and bunkers.

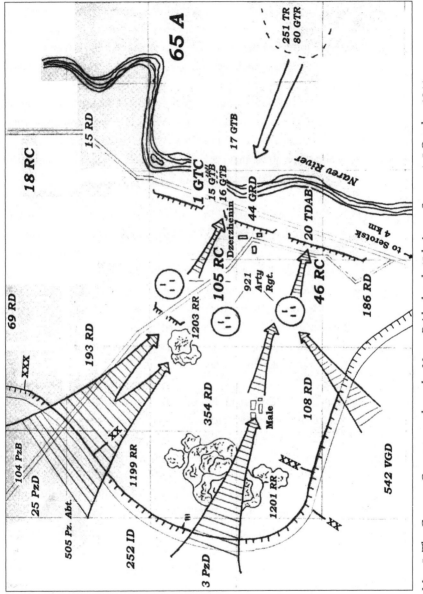

Map 5. The German Counterattack on the Narev Bridgehead, 65th Army Sector, 4–5 October 1944

Suddenly, a strong cannonade erupted. The troops of the 354th Rifle Division had never before heard or experienced such heavy artillery preparatory fire by the Germans. In just the matter of a few minutes, wire communications were severed. For a time, command over the troops at the front was lost. Radio stations operated with interruptions. The artillery preparation for the ensuing attack continued for about an hour.

Suddenly, enemy tanks appeared from beyond the Budy Tsepelenske woods. The direction of the attacks soon became clear too. The main blow was aimed at the boundary between the 193rd and 354th Rifle Divisions. One battalion of the 354th's 1199th Regiment could not withstand the initial assault and retreated. This triggered the withdrawal of both battalions of the first echelon of the 1202nd Regiment that was in reserve. The situation became serious.

By 10:00 A.M., the enemy approached the second line of our defenses. They penetrated the forward edge of this defense line around the western edge of the settlement Dzerzhenin. The settlement itself no longer existed: only shattered remnants of the buildings remained. In one such pile of rubble, the post of the division's operational group was located, headed by a deputy of Colonel Dzhandzhgava, Lieutenant Colonel Vorob'ev. He left two officers of the headquarters staff and a radio operator in the shelter of the rubble pile, while he himself ran along the trenches, rallying the retreating soldiers and putting a stop to the withdrawal of elements of the division.

Seemingly, the forward edge of our second line of our defenses was located on the reverse slope of some elevated terrain. In truth, our defenses by now had lost all depth, and our lines had collapsed into this single line of defense occupied by infantry, direct fire weapons, and batteries of self-propelled guns. They all fired simultaneously at the oncoming enemy tanks and infantry when they appeared over the crest of the slope. Uninterrupted enemy air attacks, the dense smoke, the crackle of submachine guns and machine guns, salvos of rockets—all combined to make orientation difficult. The enemy could not break through this final line of defense off the march, although they pressed against it closely.[7]

The most critical moment of the battle was between 2:00 and 4:00 P.M. The enemy made another concerted effort along the entire front to break through to the river. Here and there, individual German tanks managed to penetrate the line and headed for the riverbank. At this critical moment, the loud roar of engines and long machine-gun bursts attracted everyone's attention. Tracer rounds whistled over the heads of our infantry toward the enemy. Our heavy tanks had arrived! They drew up to the infantry's positions and stopped. From the open hatch of one tank flew a series of green signal rockets. In response, the heavy tanks' main guns roared and unleashed a powerful volley. Several of the enemy tanks erupted in flames. The tanks' gun duel continued for about forty minutes, after which the surviving, undamaged enemy tanks began to retreat. At this point, further reinforcements arrived in the form of destroyer antitank batteries and infantry from the 44th Rifle Division. The antitank guns took positions directly behind the line of our infantry's trenches. "Guards die on their gun carriages, but the enemy shall not pass"—such was their combat motto.

From the first to the last day of this battle for the bridgehead, Colonel Dzhandzhgava was always present at the most threatened points along our front. On the evening of 4 October, he had ordered his deputies to cross the river into the bridgehead and personally direct their subordinate troops. The senior radio operator for the divisional command, Senior Sergeant Konstantin Shebeko later said:

> The enemy's tanks broke through our front lines in the sector of the 1199th Regiment and closely approached the banks of the Narev in the vicinity of our crossing point. The divisional commander placed his observation post beneath the steep banks of the Narev among the guns of an antitank battalion, practically in the front lines. From this spot he observed the course of the fighting and let no one cross back to the left (east) bank of the river.

That night, a battery of SU-76 self-propelled guns crossed the river into the slender bridgehead and arrived at the divisional headquarters and Dzhandzhgava's observation post beneath the steep bank of the river. These self-propelled vehicles mounted the excellent ZIS-3 76-mm gun and carried a strong punch. They also had strong frontal armor but very thin side armor. Tarpaulin covered the top and rear of the vehicles. Because of their armor weaknesses, we called the SU-76 "Proshchai, Rodina!" ("Farewell, Motherland!"), but the crews often referred to it as "Suka" ("Bitch") in a mixture of admiration and scorn.

Approximately a kilometer away from Dzhandzhgava's observation post and the river crossing, five German Marders were positioned and firing at the river crossing and all approaches to it. Colonel Dzhandzhgava ordered the SU-76 battery commander to destroy or chase away these German armored vehicles. The commander examined the area, the position of the targets, designated a plan of battle, and set it in motion. From my vantage point, I watched as the first gun in the battery slowly began to climb the slope of the riverbank. Its gun crew loaded the main gun and prepared to take a snap shot at the Germans. But as soon as the vehicle crested the bank of the river, it was struck by a shell and burst into flames without having fired a shot. The very same misfortune befell the second gun, which had attempted the same operation. Now two of the "Sukas" were burning.

A lieutenant ran up to the battery commander and asked permission to try once again to suppress the enemy. The commander was upset with the loss of two vehicles and gave permission. The lieutenant selected a volunteer driver, gunner, and mechanic. He gave the following assignment to the driver and gunner: "At top speed, move to the right-hand burning 'Suka.' Pop up the bank just 1 meter to its right and fire. After your shot, full speed backward and bound to the left about 200 meters to that little shed. From behind it, fire at the extreme left 'Ferdinand,' then again full speed reverse and back to your right."

The driver and gunner climbed into a waiting SU-76. The other members of the crew remained below under cover of the riverbank. The small crew did exactly as the lieutenant instructed, and under partial cover from the burning vehicle, they quickly selected a target and fired. The middle Marder erupted in flames. The enemy managed to detect from where the shot had come, and opened fire on their position. But it was already empty, as the "Suka" had reversed back down the slope. While the enemy self-propelled guns continued to fire at its previous position, the SU-76 managed to reach the second position next to the shed. It quickly aimed at the left-hand Marder and set it on fire with its first shot. The enemy didn't seem to notice the new location of their tormentor, and didn't switch their fire to the little shed. So the brave little gun crew in the "Suka" decided to fire another round from this position. The right-hand Marder burst into flames. Three Marders were now burning. The remaining two

German guns managed to retreat behind the crest of a hillock and escaped. The successful crew was honored with awards and medals.

The weather improved, and our air force began appearing in greater numbers. Later that day, I was sitting near the divisional commander. A major was sitting next to him, directing the battle. Suddenly the major asked the commander, "Do you see those shrubs?" He pointed at some dense shrubs about one kilometer away from us. The commander replied, "I see them."

"And do you see those German guns under the shrubbery?"

"No, I don't see anything."

"Then what the devil are you sitting on?"

A flight of our dive-bombers quickly appeared and were directed to the target that the major had spotted. One, two, three planes went into a dive and released their bombs. The German battery was eliminated.

Things became easier for us. The German "Ferdinands" had retreated, and the battery had been destroyed. That night, the 37th Guards Rifle Division came up. The pressure from the enemy eased, as the Germans sensed that we had received some reinforcements. Colonel Dzhandzhgava rearranged his lines, shifting the 1201st Rifle Regiment, which had been on the extreme left flank, over to the extreme right. With the assistance of the 37th Guards Rifle Division, we gradually pushed the Germans back up to four kilometers and reestablished our former defensive positions in the bridgehead. The crisis had passed, but the fighting for the bridgehead continued until 10 October.

Once the fighting for the bridgehead ended, the commander of the 473rd Transportation Battalion received an order to release immediately fourteen men to the headquarters of the division. The division was sweeping the rear area for replacements for the frontline units. I was among the fourteen. We were seen off with obvious sorrow: our comrades had a foreboding for what awaited us.

At the collecting point, in addition to us, there were already 200 men. They grouped the 14 of us into one platoon. The guys in my platoon knew that I had circulated among the upper echelon, that I knew many officers, and they began to ask me to go to the division's chief of staff and remind him of a Stalin order that forbade turning soldiers and sergeants with special skills, such as drivers and machinists, into frontline infantry. I didn't want to stick my neck out, but they compelled me. The lieutenant colonel heard me out. Then he abruptly barked the command, "Fall in!"

As I headed back to my platoon, I spotted a driver who was leaving to go see Major Chirkin. I asked him to hand a note from me to Chirkin, that let him know that they were sending us off to the infantry as regular soldiers. The driver set off, and we began to fall into line. Several senior officers of the headquarters arrived to accompany the new reinforcements to the front line. Altogether there were 400 of us in the column, and we headed out to the accompaniment of a brass band. An officer in the political department, an acquaintance of mine named Butsol, caught sight of me in the column and promised to look into the matter.

We arrived at the front lines and took a short rest. Then we moved out to replace the worn-out units in the front line. We immediately set to improving the entrenchments and building positions for our heavy machine guns.

We spent a week in the front lines. Back in the trenches again, I became something of a mentor and guardian to the young Kiselov, one of the new chauffeurs that had arrived the previous month as replacements. I taught him many tips on how to stay alive at the front, and how one should conduct oneself in combat conditions.

The Germans undertook nothing serious during this period. Then a fortified district unit arrived to replace us.[8] They had plenty of machine guns and took over our sector of the front, while our regiment was withdrawn to draw replacements and reform.

Major Chirkin Intercedes

When we returned to the rear area, Major Chirkin intervened to free me from my frontline service with the infantry. He didn't have permission to keep me for himself, but he also didn't want to release me to a position far removed from him. Temporarily, while he waited permission to have a motorcyclist assigned to him, Major Chirkin sent me to serve in the repair platoon of the 921st Artillery Regiment. He didn't want to return me to the transportation battalion, because there the deputy divisional commander could grab me again to drive his Willys and then it would be very difficult for Chirkin to get me back. On 5 November 1944, Order 059 assigned me as a driver to the 921st Artillery Regiment.

The regiment's repair platoon consisted of thirteen men, under the command of a senior sergeant. The platoon was busy with repairs and the preparation of heavy equipment, prime movers, and vehicles for winter operations. We were overhauling engines and stripping the still useful parts from engines that had reached the end of their service. We also compiled records that detailed the defects found by our engine inspections, and together with the defective parts sent them to the 65th Army's master repairmen. Besides drawing up these diagnostic reports, I also was the platoon's cook. Our breakfasts were later than usual, since I could not manage to prepare them by 7:00 A.M. Therefore the other guys in the platoon would go to work, and within about an hour I would call them to breakfast. From 9:00 to 11:00 A.M., I worked on the defect reports, and then I would begin to prepare lunch. From 1:00 P.M. until 5:00 P.M., I did my repair duties again, and then fixed dinner. Our group was small and friendly. But my service here in the artillery regiment was brief.

On 14 November, I was sitting together with the senior sergeant, putting together the inventory records, when the telephone suddenly rang. Major Chirkin was calling. Chirkin informed me that the divisional commander had been given a Willys, and he had asked him, Chirkin, to pick an experienced driver for it. Chirkin proposed that I work for a while with the divisional commander, until they could find an experienced, suitable replacement. Recalling my unhappy experience with informal requests and assignments that led to my arrest for desertion, I hesitated, but Chirkin persisted until I agreed. That very day, Chirkin delivered me to the rear area of the division, and together with the chief of the automotive services, on the morning of 15 November, we set off for the division's command post.

With the 354th Rifle Division's Commander, V. N. Dzhandzhgava

We reached the headquarters safely. It was located on the right bank of the Narev River, about eight kilometers from the river and just beyond the Serotsk-Pultusk road. There were several bunkers here, in which all the basic services of the division's headquarters were located: the operations center, the artillery commander, the chief of reconnaissance, a bunker for the divisional commander himself, a bunker for the headquarters security platoon, and one for the commander's personal staff. Everything was superbly camouflaged.

Upon arrival at the command post, I dropped by the bunker in which the commander's personal driver and radioman were living. Among my old acquaintances there, I found only Senior Sergeant Kostia Alekhin, who I had replaced the previous summer. He had recovered from his wounds a long time ago and continued his service as driver for his previous vehicle. He showed me the division's Willys.

By appearance, the jeep was clearly not fresh off the assembly line. I looked everything over, checked the carburetor, started up the engine, put it in gear, and started forward. The steering wheel was badly worn and cut, and the brakes worked poorly. I couldn't do anything about them at the moment, as the brakes were hydraulic, and I didn't have any brake fluid with me. I reported my findings to Chirkin and gave him my estimate for how quickly I could make the repairs.

The chief of the automotive services reported to the divisional commander about the transfer of the Willys, and the commander announced that they would now leave to take Chirkin back to his post in the division's rear. I prepared the Willys for the trip, and within about an hour and a half, Dzhandzhgava's adjutant walked up and ordered me to drive the Willys up to the commander's bunker for departure. I pulled the jeep up directly in front of the bunker. Driver Senior Sergeant Kostia Alekhin, Sergeant Roman Trushin, Lance Corporal Mai, and Major Chirkin climbed into it. Then Colonel Dzhandzhgava, wearing a black Cossack felt coat, and his personal adjutant stepped out of the commander's bunker. The divisional commander sat next to me in the jeep, looked me over attentively, and said, "Ah . . . the Siberian . . . you've returned? You won't run away again from me, will you?"

We headed to the rear, or more precisely, to a bathhouse. The sauna was at the medical-sanitary battalion's location. All the way, Alekhin and the divisional commander swapped stories. We reached the bathhouse quickly.

After I had dressed following my bath, Lance Corporal Mai walked up to me. He was older than any of us and drove the headquarters' GAZ truck. Instead of a body, the truck had a cabin in which all the commander's personal belongings were kept and carried. This truck was rarely used, so Mai had a lot of free time, which he spent as the headquarters' backup orderly. The first orderly was Anton Piradze. Anton was often away on official business for the divisional commander, and Mai took his place while he was gone. Mai was a wise and experienced man, a Jew by nationality.[9]

Mai told me how the commander loved to travel: quickly and to brake sharply. I learned this myself on the return journey to the headquarters. We sped along, as fast as the military roads, dampened with rain, would permit. The journey passed by to merry laughter over Dzhandzhgava's anecdotes. The road to the headquarters turned into a straight and level lane about ninety meters from the commander's bunker. I sped up the jeep to about twenty miles per hour. The commander was sitting nearly sideways, with his right side toward the front windshield. When the jeep reached the bunker's entrance, I stomped on the brakes. The commander wasn't expecting this, couldn't brace himself in time, and the inertial force threw him forward. He struck his forehead on the front glass. At the moment of impact, his tall Caucasian sheepskin cap flew from his head onto the jeep's hood (the cabin was not covered with tarp).

I was terrified. The guys in the back stopped laughing. The commander looked at me sternly, and it seemed that he was ready to tear me to pieces. He looked at me fiercely for two to three seconds, which seemed to me like an hour. Then he smiled, clapped me on the right shoulder, and said, "Good man! Always stop that way!" I also smiled, and all the guys broke into laughter again. Then suddenly Dzhandzhgava stopped smiling, leaned a little toward me, and asked, "Were you afraid of me just then?" I weakly answered, "No." Then he said, "You know who is afraid of me? Those who don't give a fig about their duties are the ones who fear me." Thus began my second tour of duty with the divisional commander of the 354th Rifle Division.

At the moment of my arrival at divisional headquarters, the commander had four vehicles:

1. GAZ-A with a rear cabin, driver Mai. This was a mobile "depot."
2. GAZ-57, a Soviet-made "Willys," driver Kostia Alekhin, born 1913. His vehicle was used for trips to the rear.

3. Opel Kapitan, a captured German car, driver Roman Trushin, born approximately 1910. The divisional commander would choose this car to travel to corps' headquarters or army headquarters from time to time, but only along good roads. He also chose this car sometimes for trips to the bathhouse.

4. Willys—my vehicle. The commander traveled in it, primarily, to frontline regiments and battalions, usually in bad weather or over bad roads. My jeep was jokingly called "the troop horse," and the guys jokingly called me "Nikolai the Martyr," since I had to travel a lot virtually every day and always through the worst conditions.

In addition, the divisional commander had two radiomen, Kostia Shibeko and his assistant Volodia. Dzhandzhgava also had a cook, Sasha; a medical sergeant, Mariia Kuz'minichna Baturova, who in the past had earned the medal "Za otvagu" ("For Courage") as a company nurse; and two sentries whose names I cannot now remember.

On the second day of my service with the divisional commander, the adjutant ordered me to drive to get a replacement uniform. My uniform was filthy, covered with grease and oil spots from my time at the artillery regiment's repair platoon, and I had found no place to wash it. They fitted me for a new, clean uniform and I began to look like a divisional commander's chauffeur!

On the third and fourth day of my service, we visited the commander of our neighboring division, the 193rd Rifle Division, on his birthday: Hero of the Soviet Union Major General A. G. Frolenkov. While there, I became acquainted with my colleague chauffeurs and drivers from other divisions. The visit to this Hero of the Soviet Union's headquarters was a good omen, as sometime before the first of December, I brought to Dzhandzhgava his first general's uniform. For his successful defense of the Narev bridgehead in October 1944, Colonel Dzhandzhgava was awarded the title "Hero of the Soviet Union" and promoted to major general.

At the end of November or the beginning of December 1944, the third anniversary of the formation of our division was widely celebrated. At the time of the party, both the Germans and we were standing in defensive postures, and therefore we had the opportunity to celebrate this anniversary properly. Some of the festivities occurred in the division's underground club on the right bank of the Narev River. There were guests from neighboring divisions: tank men, artillerists, corps commanders, and the 65th Army's commanding general Batov, who spent about an hour at the celebration then left, while all the rest partied until midnight. Altogether, there were about 300 people at the celebration. I best of all recall a major there, who was the chief of staff for a tank brigade.

Before the New Year of 1945, our army fell back under command of the Second Belorussian Front and its commander became our previous *front* commander, Marshal Rokossovskii. The troops of our Second Belorussian Front and our neighboring Third Belorussian Front had the joint task of destroying the enemy's East Prussian group, which had the ability to threaten our forces advancing on Berlin.

Chapter 7

The Final Offensive

About 5 January 1945, the commander of the 65th Army, Colonel General P. I. Batov, paid a visit to our division. Together with Dzhandzhgava, they went to examine the place that had been designated for the breakthrough of the enemy's defenses in the coming offensive.

The generals were dressed in sheepskin coats and wearing simple officer's caps on their heads. There were no shoulder straps on their coats. The adjutants remained at the divisional command post while I drove the officers to the front lines. As I drove, the generals talked about the forthcoming offensive, about the preparations for it, and about possible start dates. I overheard Batov telling Dzhandzhgava: "You know, some Americans in the Ardennes have turned chicken and buggered off nearly 300 kilometers to the rear. Churchill has asked Stalin, 'For God's sake, start your offensive sooner.' We'll have to start our offensive a week earlier. We must have everything ready." In this way, I learned that the Stavka had moved up the start date for our offensive.[1]

The designated breakthrough spot was opposite one of our antitank battalions. I parked the jeep, and while the generals talked with the artillerists, I tucked the divisional commander's map case under my arm, and in the role of an adjutant, I headed up a communications trench toward the front line. I walked about 200 meters from the Willys and stopped, waiting for the generals and hoping that they would permit me to accompany them to the front line. The generals left the artillerists and walked up to me. General Dzhandzhgava took his map case from me and sent me back to the Willys. I asked permission to go with them to the front, but he refused: "There is nothing for you to do there, and the Germans already have enough targets up there without you."

I returned to the jeep and waited, while the generals made their observations, then walked around the trenches, bunkers, and gun pits, checking out the soldiers' readiness and morale. While I waited, I sat down with some fellows and told them, "You know, there's a commotion back at divisional headquarters. Someone is firing at the

Germans, but neither our scouts nor the Germans can figure out where the firing is coming from."

I looked at them. The guys in the group exchanged glances, grinned, and then took me to show who was firing. When the Germans had retreated following their early October attack, we took over some of their positions and combined them into our new defensive line. Some soldiers found a place where a few German "Vaniushi" had been positioned, six-barreled rocket launchers that brayed like donkeys when they hurled their rounds toward us. As soon as we heard the distinct sound of a "Vaniusha" firing, we immediately shouted, "Brothers, a donkey! Take cover!" This meant that rockets were now headed our way, and that soon there would be explosions. When the Germans had retreated, they had left behind piles of these rockets—it seemed, as many as had been delivered to the position. Our soldiers had found them and thought to give them a try. They would take a rocket, lay it on the breastwork of the trench, and then fire at this percussion cap at the base of the rocket with their *avtomat*. The rocket would explode, and the shell would fly off in the general direction of the German lines. Therefore the Germans could not figure out from where the fire was coming.

When the generals had returned from their visit to the front line, I told them about the "disturbers of the peace." General Batov said, "Well, show us." The guys and their sergeant showed them on the spot how they "fired" the rockets. Batov said, "I don't have anything in my pocket. I only have this Order of the Red Star. I award it to the sergeant for coming up with this 'technique' of harassing the enemy. Award the remaining troops yourself, Vladimir Nikolaevich [Dzhandzhgava], under your own authority." I returned to the Willys, and the generals came back later, at sunset, and we headed back to the 354th's command post.

During this lull in combat operations following the failure of the German counteroffensive against the Narev bridgehead in October 1944, both sides prepared for the coming Soviet winter offensive. The race to prepare was uneven—German reinforcement and resupply of the Eastern Front units were constrained by Hitler's planned Ardennes offensive in the West, and the Allied heavy bombing campaign was finally beginning to take its toll on German fuel supplies. By now, the Stavka had become quite adept at marshaling tremendous superiorities in troops and equipment at points of intended breakthroughs, and such was the case for Rokossovskii's Second Belorussian Front in its Pultusk and Serotsk bridgeheads across the Narev. A German staff officer who served in a panzer division during this campaign later estimated that the Second Belorussian Front had superiorities of 7:1 in infantry, 18:1 in artillery, and 10 to 12:1 in armor along the Pultusk/Serotsk sector of the front.[2]

Into the Pultusk and Serotsk bridgeheads, Rokossovskii's Second Belorussian Front had jammed two combined arms armies, the 65th and the 70th, and one armored corps, the 1st Guards "Don" Tank Corps. This corps normally operated with the 65th Army and would do so again in the coming offensive. Significantly, the Stavka had also successfully transferred the 5th Tank Army to Rokossovskii's front without detection by the Germans. However, this tank army operated north of Litvin's army out of the Rozan bridgehead, and although it was the dominant operating force of the Second Belorussian Front during the East Prussia offensive, it does not figure in Litvin's narrative.

In the trenches opposite Rokossovskii's Second Belorussian Front was a familiar opponent—the German Second Army, the same army (on paper at least) that it had ruptured and battered on its way to the Dnepr River in August 1943. But now the Second Army was perhaps even weaker, as most of its replacements were men with little or even no training. The German divisions opposing the 65th Army's breakout from the Narev were part of the German XXVII Army Corps. From south to north, they consisted of the 542nd, the 252nd, and the 35th Infantry Divisions.

The defensive lines around the Pultusk bridgehead were dense but rather thinly manned. There were four belts of defensive works. The first, constructed by the troops themselves, consisted of three layered trench lines with a depth of one and a half to two kilometers. Two kilometers behind this first line of works was a second line, which sheltered the divisional artillery. Two to four kilometers behind that was a third line of trenches, which lay in front of an antitank ditch fronting a line of antitank obstacles. A fourth line of defenses lay about twelve kilometers from the forward edge of battle. A civil heavy engineering battalion built the remaining lines behind the first line.[3]

These lines of fortifications would have offered a stiff defense against the Soviet offensive, had the Germans possessed adequate manpower to man them. However, in January 1945, this was rarely possible anywhere. On the Pultusk front, for example, the German 252nd Division had only two regiments with approximately 1,000 noncommissioned officers and men to cover twelve kilometers of front.[4]

Of serious concern to the Second Army headquarters was the fact that it had only one division in reserve, the 7th Panzer Division. It was situated in the area of Ciechanow, astride the boundary between the Second Army's XXVII and XXIII Corps. On the eve of the Soviet offensive, according to an estimate of its commander, the 7th Panzer Division only had about two-thirds of its regulation tank strength. About half of these tanks were the Mk V "Panther," and the remaining ones were the older Mk IV tanks. While the divisional commander considered the esprit de corps of all personnel as "good," there were serious shortages of fuel and ammunition that hampered the division's operational effectiveness.[5]

The Stavka's plan for Rokossovskii's Second Belorussian Front in the coming offensive was to break out of the Pultusk, Serotsk, and Rozan bridgeheads, then head generally in a west-by-northwest direction to grab bridgeheads over the Vistula River between Marienburg in the north and Kulm in the south. From this point, it was less clear where the Second Belorussian Front would head, as the Stavka expected the Germans in East Prussia to fall back quickly to the Baltic coastline. Thus, Rokossovskii's Front lay exposed to the possibility of pursuing divergent aims: the encirclement of East Prussia or the advance on Berlin. For the time being, however, the 65th and 70th Armies on Second Belorussian Front's southern flank were to advance generally westward, maintaining cooperation with the north wing of Marshal Zhukov's First Belorussian Front as it advanced west from Warsaw.

Forward!

By 10 January 1945, there had been some command changes in the 354th Rifle Division. Colonel Vorob'ev, the division's deputy commander for combat construction, had been promoted out of the division. Colonel Strunin arrived to take over in his place. Colonel Grokhovskii, our division's artillery commander, had also been promoted to a corps-level position.

On 13 January at twilight, I brought to the observation post the divisional commander and his operations group, which consisted of his chief of operations, Lieutenant Colonel Os'kina, the chief of reconnaissance, and the artillery commander. The observation post had been established at the edge of a forest, sixty meters from the front line, not far from a bunker of the 25th Assault Battalion. I drove the officers and generals to the middle of the forest, in which the observation post was positioned, and they walked the rest of the way on foot. Before they left, General Dzhandzhgava gave me an order to bring them breakfast the next morning, 14 January, by 9:00 A.M. The officers left, and I helped antitank crews move three 76-mm guns into position on the front line, where they could fire over open sights at enemy positions. The gun crews were rolling their guns forward by hand, and they were delighted to have a tow from my jeep. Within an hour, I had towed all three guns into position on the front line.

The night of 13–14 January was restless. No one slept much. Artillery gun tubes, and "Katiusha" and "Andriusha"[6] rocket launchers were rolling toward the line of departure. Everyone was moving into their positions and preparing for battle. Infantry regiments occupied the forward trenches. Everyone's mood—from the lowest foot soldier to the general himself—was elevated: everyone was ready for the decisive battle.

For nearly three months after the end of the battle for the Narev bridgehead, we had used the relative calm to prepare for another offensive, which we hoped would be the final one of the war. Units received replacements and fresh supplies, and conducted active training of the soldiers to prepare them for combat. On several occasions, we trained under live ammunition. High-explosive shells would be fired at soldiers huddled in their trenches. The explosions would shower the trenches with dirt and fragments, and there were even cases of wounds and deaths among the trainees. We also trained in individual antitank combat. At these training sessions, soldiers would crouch in trenches, over which tanks would pass. The tanks would make several small turns over the trenches, and then continue on their way toward the rear. The soldiers would then rise up and toss training grenades at the rear of the tanks. In this fashion, the soldiers were taught to endure the fear of shellfire and tanks.

Before the offensive, the number of scouts and reconnaissance units had increased by three to five times, and a competition for the right to be assigned to the scouts had originated at this time. Everyone who had distinguished themselves in the preceding battles had been awarded their honors and medals, and before the offensive, all of them had been given a period of rest in the division's rear area rest and recreation quarters. The artillerists had been amazed that ammunition had not been denied to them; on the contrary, they had received more shells than they had requested. Everyone in the line units was warmly dressed and had received a warm meal before the battle.

At 8:00 A.M. on 14 January 1945, I dropped by the cook and reminded him for the third time that the general's and officers' breakfast was late. The preparatory artillery bombardment was due to begin at 11:00 A.M., and the road between the swamps leading to the front line was full of tanks. It would be impossible for us to reach the command post on time, once the tanks were moving forward. Sasha didn't have something ready, and we didn't arrive at the command post with breakfast until 10:30 A.M., which provoked some indignation in the divisional commander. Having eaten as quickly as possible, the general and officers took their positions and prepared to conduct the battle. Sasha and I gathered up the dishes into two heavy cardboard boxes. We each took one of the boxes and hurried toward the Willys, which was parked about 300 meters away next to the 25th Assault Battalion's bunker. The deputy divisional commander for rear services was supposed to come with us.

With our dishes, we ran through the forest toward the jeep. As I ran, I saw soldiers holding shells in their hands by their mortar tubes, and artillerists were standing by their loaded barrels, holding the firing cords. We had run about halfway to the Willys when I heard the first three reports from the guns which I had helped tow into position the night before. For the next fleeting second, it was possible to hear individual guns being fired, and then everything merged into one combined nightmarish roar, the likes of which I had never before heard. Thus began our preparatory bombardment.[7]

My head soon began to spin from the boom of the discharging artillery pieces. I thought for a moment about those on the receiving end of these shells sent by an entire armada of guns standing in three ranks along the entire front. I stopped by the gun pit of one of our 82-mm mortars. I stood there with the eyes of a drunken man. The mortar battery commander, a senior lieutenant who I knew from his time in the reserve, spotted my senseless face, grabbed me by the belt around my sheepskin coat, and yanked me down into a trench. Not far away, enemy shells and mortar rounds began to explode.

After about forty minutes, I left the shelter of the hospitable mortar men and headed for the jeep, in order to get away before the tanks began moving. I ran up to the car and found Sasha already there, but the lieutenant colonel was missing. We waited for what seemed an interminable time until he finally appeared, and we set off on our way. About halfway back, we ran into a column of tanks moving toward us. I had to turn off the road to the right, into a frozen swamp, and drive through it.

Along the road, the tanks of Lieutenant Colonel Pustukhov were passing westward to our left. In front of them were eight minesweeping tanks. These had toothed heavy rollers, one meter wider than the tanks, attached by hinges to the front of each tank. Passing through an enemy minefield, the heavy rollers would explode the mines. Upon each mine explosion, the blast would fling the mine sweep upward on its hinges, and under its own weight, the mine sweep would fall back into position in front of the tank.

We continued eastward through the frozen muck of the swamp until I reached a traverse trench for a 152-mm battery. The trench blocked our way, so I turned again to the right and drove parallel to the trench, trying to find some way across or around it. German shells began exploding nearby. We abandoned the jeep and jumped into the trench. We crawled along the trench for a short distance, enemy shells erupting around us. I looked around and saw a place where our vehicle could get across about fifty meters up ahead. I turned around and crawled back to the Willys. The enemy continued its barrage from long-range artillery. It was apparent that they had targeted this particular 152-mm battery standing beside the road for counterbattery fire.

When I reached a point in the trench opposite my Willys, I stopped and analyzed the enemy's fire pattern. The enemy's shells were falling and exploding every thirty seconds. I lay in the bottom of the trench, so that if a shell struck my Willys and overturned it, the jeep would not crush me.

I decided to get back into the jeep and drive to the gap I had spotted in the transverse trench. I crawled up to the Willys, and not abandoning my embrace of the earth, reached in and started the engine up, then waited for the next shell explosion. It soon arrived and scattered shell fragments and clods of earth all around me. I jumped into the jeep and drove along the trench. Ahead and to the right another shell burst quite nearby. I felt a blow against my vehicle, but it was no time to stop, and the jeep kept moving, so I still had all I needed to save my skin. I swerved the jeep through the gap in the trenches, then turned sharply left and drove back toward the road. The final tank in the column was passing in front of me. The tank men waved me good-bye and continued toward the front lines. I exited onto the road, turned toward the command post, and searched for my passengers. I drove slowly. I came upon the deputy divisional commander first, and then Sasha jumped out of a roadside ditch. The entire crew was together again, and we drove to the command post. There I closely examined the Willys and found six holes. The front windshield was also shattered.

Once the preparatory artillery bombardment had begun, approximately ten of our scouts from the division's scout company crawled out of the forward trenches, then stood up and walked at full height across no-man's-land toward the enemy front line. Having gone no farther than 100 meters, they stopped and waited a little until the artillery had shifted fire to the second line of trenches. At this point, they rushed forward into the enemy trenches and even before the end of the artillery bombardment, returned to our lines with the first enemy prisoners. The prisoners were alive but looked like corpses: they themselves could not believe that they were still alive after such a barrage.

The artillery preparatory bombardment lasted for one and a half hours. The artillery concentrated on command and observation posts of the enemy, supply depots, and strongly fortified field positions. "Katiusha" and "Andriusha" rocket launchers spread destruction across the belts of the enemy's defensive posture. The infantry went on the attack within a half hour of the start of the bombardment, following the walking barrage into the depths of the enemy's position. Infantry support guns, Su-76 self-propelled guns, and other direct-fire weapons closely followed the advancing infantry. They targeted enemy machine-gun nests and antitank gun positions, and thereby permitted the infantry's successful advance. On the first day of the offensive, we reached the third belt of the enemy's fortifications.[8]

Within three hours after the start of the offensive, medium-caliber artillery batteries and all mortar batteries were redeploying forward. By the end of the first day of action, our regiments had advanced up to eight kilometers. The divisional commander moved his observation post forward about six kilometers.

The fighting was difficult, and poor weather conditions hampered the activity of our close support aircraft. After the third day of fighting, the enemy's main forces had been crushed and scattered. Once it had successfully punched through the enemy's fortifications in depth, our division's advance gained speed, fighting primarily against strong rearguard elements of the enemy.

On 18 January, the 354th Rifle Division participated in the capture of the Polish city of Plonsk. The Germans had mined all approaches to the city, and it required hard fighting to clear the city. One sector of trenches changed hands six times. When the battle ended, the Stavka awarded the honorific designation "Plonsk" to the 1199th Rifle Regiment of the 354th Rifle Division.[9]

Over the next twelve days, our division advanced approximately 200 kilometers. The weather had cleared and remained dry, frosty, and a little windy. As in the summer before, a mobile detachment spearheaded our advance. These mobile forward elements moved round the clock, giving the enemy no time to stop, rest, or fortify. Without sufficient strength to seal off our breakthrough, the enemy brought up whatever forces it had at hand to try and slow us down: security battalions, Volksturm [people's militia] battalions, and other lightly equipped, poorly trained units.[10]

At the Animal Husbandry Farm

After about a week since the start of the offensive, our division was moving in mobile columns behind the forward detachments. We spent the night at some rich German's estate, and we marveled at the luxurious accommodations. We resumed our travels early the next morning. Only the general, his adjutant, his radiomen, sentries, and I were in the jeep. Our destination was the next command post, which was due to be liberated by our troops by the middle of the day.

By 9:00 A.M., we had caught up with our forward detachment, which had been reinforced with artillery and a cavalry squadron. The forward detachment had halted in a large village next to the fence of an alcohol factory. The soldiers were eating breakfast. The divisional commander ordered the officer in charge of the advance guard to immediately resume his designated advance, once the troops had finished breakfast. General Dzhandzhgava also was curious about the location of the cavalry squadron. The commander of the advance guard reported that the cavalrymen had left an hour ago along the route of advance, and that he was waiting for a dispatch from them. General Dzhandzhgava told him not to wait any longer, and ordered him to resume his advance in the expectation of catching up with or encountering the returning cavalry and to learn from them the situation further along the route of advance.

We left the village and drove about 6 kilometers without meeting any of our cavalry. We stopped on a small rise and examined our surroundings. Ahead, about 6 or 7 kilometers west of us lay a village with about seventy buildings lying on either side of a single street. About 800 meters closer to us was some sort of farm or agricultural enterprise. We could see residences and outbuildings. It turned out to be a small animal husbandry farm with premises for keeping fodder and animals, farm implements, and people's dwellings. Almost all the buildings were brick, with red tile roofs. We could not see our cavalry squadron anywhere up ahead.

According to the evening intelligence reports from our scouts, the village was in enemy hands. Dzhandzhgava ordered weapons to be readied, and to move forward to the farm, to wait at first for our cavalrymen, then to decide what to do next. I pushed the windshield down on the hood and placed a captured submachine gun on the dashboard, pointing forward. The radiomen readied their personal weapons, the sentries—their own, and the adjutant prepared a machine gun.

We reached the farm safely and drove into the courtyard. The sentries took up positions around the yard. Inside the main residence were two Poles. They were frightened when they spotted a large Soviet general, wearing a Cossack's felt cloak, enter the room in which they were cowering. The Poles said that a German transportation company with approximately 150 carts/vehicles and 200 soldiers and officers was situated in the village down the road. As they told it, approximately twenty minutes ago, two horse-drawn carts with Germans had left the farm. From the Germans' conversation, said the Poles, it was clear that the Germans were planning to abandon the village and continue their retreat. However, probabilities didn't exclude the possible return of the Germans to the farm, so Dzhandzhgava ordered a circular defense of the building to be established. We set up the machine gun in a window facing the village and positioned the sentries and one of the radiomen around the courtyard. The other radioman established a connection with the corps commander, who rebuked Dzhandzhgava for his lack of caution and ordered him to pull back from the farm. However, Dzhandzhgava persuaded the corps commander to allow him to remain in his present position.

After the negotiations with the corps commander, Dzhandzhgava contacted the commander of the advance guard and ordered one reinforced company to make a rapid march to the village. Suddenly, the second radioman ran into the room and reported that some sort of turretless tank was moving toward our farm. We readied our antitank reserve, two antitank grenades, for action and prepared for battle. This tank entered the courtyard and turned out to be a T-34, without a turret but with a bow machine gun. The head of a tank man popped out of the tank—it was one of ours. It turned out to be a tractor-tank from the 1st Guards Tank Corps. The vehicle's commander told the general that he was driving around in search of knocked-out or immobilized tanks to dismantle them for useful parts, or to give them a tow back for repairs. The general explained the situation to the tank commander and told him that it was desirable not to let any Germans escape the village alive. The general asked the tank commander to drive around the village, enter it from the west, and to destroy the German column with machine-gun fire and its treads upon encountering it. Just after the tank left, the cavalry appeared. The divisional commander assigned it to attack from the east, as soon as it heard firing from the western edge of the village.

The plan went off without a hitch. Within about twenty minutes, the German column had been destroyed. The cavalrymen took about thirty prisoners and brought them to the divisional commander. Less than half the prisoners were Germans; the remainder was made up of Yugoslavs, Poles, and others.

For the successful conduct of this battle, the divisional commander awarded the tank crew with honors and medals. During the war, divisional commanders had been given the right in the name of the USSR Supreme Soviet to honor those who had distinguished themselves in action right up to the Order of the Red Star, but to commanding officers of the units involved, only up to the "Za otvagu" medal.

On 26 January, the men of the division reached the Vistula River a little southwest of the Fortress Graudenz,[11] at a point where the river resumes its northerly flow toward the Baltic. That morning, under cover of thick fog, elements of our 1199th and 2003rd Rifle Regiments, with a battery of 45-mm guns, were able to seize a bridgehead on the western bank, but the ice was too thin to support tanks or artillery.[12] Shvydkov, the commander of our engineering-sapper battalion, ordered the ice to be thickened by diverting the water from a nearby canal over it. Unfortunately, the weather turned unexpectedly warm, which weakened the ice further and frustrated our efforts to cross the whole division over the Vistula. While infantry held the bridgehead on the western shore, the division's tanks and artillery remained on the eastern shore, along with our divisional rear area. We spent almost a week on the Vistula before we were able to get some tanks and artillery across it.

While we waited for nature to cooperate, our command post spent three days and nights in some Polish village to the east of the Vistula, not far from the bridgehead. We, the drivers, were billeted in the Polish home of the Rakoshinskii family, which consisted of the father, his wife, and their daughter, Vikhtia. Vikhtia was about my own age, and planned to be a schoolteacher. I spent a lot of time together with Vikhtia. She was very surprised to meet a genuine Siberian, because she had always imagined Siberians as half-men/half-beasts, and Siberia itself as some sort of wild frontier. We conversed a lot with the family—primarily about collective farms, because the Poles feared that we were bringing collectivization with us. Vikhtia also sang love songs in a beautiful voice, and these were some of my most pleasant days during the war.

Around the end of January, as we were still trying to get our entire force across the Vistula, we received a surprising order: "Dzhandzhgava, bring one of your regiments back across the river—a 10,000-man German force is moving toward the rear of the 65th Army along the eastern bank." The large group of Germans was fleeing Torun, trying to escape encirclement.[13] At this time, our three rifle regiments and some light artillery had crossed the Vistula, but our division's rear area and much of the artillery was still on the right bank, exposed to the German advance. Dzhandzhgava immediately

118 withdrew the 1199th Rifle Regiment from the Vistula bridgehead and, in concert with elements of the 193rd Rifle Division and other units, destroyed the German force. More than 7,000 Germans were taken prisoner.

With the threat neutralized, we returned our focus to crossing our entire force to the left bank of the Vistula. Once this was accomplished, our division was redirected to the north, toward Danzig. The Danzig fortified sector lay in our path, and we had the task to reach it before the enemy could attempt to occupy it. The weather became warm, almost springlike, though it was still only February. We used all measures in order to advance as quickly as possible. The Fortress Graudenz remained in our rear, but we left behind sufficient force to lay siege to the city and to compel its eventual surrender.

As the German Second Army withdrew to the Vistula, its recent reinforcement, the 83rd Infantry Division, fell back upon Graudenz. For the first two weeks of February, the 83rd Infantry Division, together with the so-called Herman Goering Replacement Brigade, attempted to hold the city as a bridgehead across the Vistula on Second Army's left flank. It had only the most tenuous connection to its neighboring division across the Vistula to the west, the 252nd Infantry Division. Eventually, pressure forced the 252nd to retreat to the north. On 15 February, the Second Army instructed the 83rd Division to abandon Graudenz and join the withdrawal. However, Hitler rescinded this order, as he had declared Graudenz a "fortress" from which withdrawal was forbidden. After a protest by the Second Army commander, Hitler permitted part of the 83rd Division and the Herman Goering Replacement Brigade to leave, but he ordered that one regiment from each unit must remain in the city, to defend it together with a number of Volksturm units. In a stubborn but ultimately misguided defense, the Graudenz garrison held out against the Soviet siege for six weeks, before capitulating on 8 March after three weeks of vicious house-to-house fighting inside the city.[14]

At the Count's Estate

As we advanced toward Danzig, I recall that our command post once spent forty-eight hours at the estate of a certain count, who was absent at the time, serving with the German army. This was a corner of paradise, surrounded by a planted forest. A stone wall enclosed the estate. A three-story residence built of white stone stood within the courtyard. A Roman Catholic church with a splendid organ stood beside the manor house. The estate was entirely deserted, but just in case, Kostia Alekhin and I took our pistols when we went to examine the manor. It was magnificent, with examples of ancient weaponry and medieval armor. A black-and-white portrait of Hitler was hanging on one wall. Kostia proposed that we have a little target practice, and so we did. Each of us fired three times, but never once struck the face. I was preparing to fire a fourth time, when General Dzhandzhgava approached us. He gently scolded us for our lousy shooting with our own personal sidearms, pulled a captured Mauser out of his holster, and fired a shot at the portrait. The bullet plowed directly into Hitler's forehead.

Looking over the church with Kostia, we found everything inside untouched. This was surprising, because the Germans always plundered such churches, carrying away valuable icons, gilded chandeliers, and other church utensils. We didn't touch anything inside the church. An enormous organ occupied one wall of the church. The diameter of its largest pipe was larger than thirty centimeters, and its height was more than ten meters. Kostia knew how to play the piano and sat down behind the keyboard. He pressed some keys, but no sound followed. Kostia pushed a button containing the inscription "Motor," but the motor didn't start: there was no electricity. I had to go to the muscular bellows and pump air into the organ. Once the air arrived, Kostia tried to play the famous Russian dance tune "Komarinskii," but couldn't manage it. This fervent dance was not suited to the organ's tender and drawn-out notes. Next he began to play Bach. The majestic sounds of this melody drew General Dzhandzhgava's attention, and he strolled into the church. He asked Kostia to play a well-known Georgian song, "Suliko." Kostia sang one couplet in Russian, and Dzhandzhgava, one couplet in Georgian. Kostia then played a famous Georgian dance tune, "Lezginka," to which Dzhandzhgava danced superbly! I had seen him perform this dance the first time at a SMERSH celebration in the village of Vul'sk-Zatorsk, the second time at the third anniversary party for the division, and a third time while visiting General Frolenkov.

In the palace's chests of drawers, we discovered many high-quality clothes. The adjutant allowed us to select a few needed items and send them back to our families as gifts. We did this with joy. I sent

120   one suit and one overcoat to each of my two younger brothers, who were working in military factories. Later, whenever we uncovered some booty, the commander gave us permission to send one package home each month, weighing no more than ten kilograms. I sent home items in short supply, primarily clothing, because during the war it was impossible to find replacements for worn-out clothes.

As we had moved through Polish territory beyond the Narev River, we seldom encountered any civilians. We were constantly advancing, and in general had neither the time nor the intent to disturb the local population. There were occasional cases when one of our officers went missing: someone somewhere found lodging for the night, someone dropped behind and "disappeared" for a while.

The situation changed once the troops of the Red Army entered German territory. A strong desire for retribution arose in many of them, after the years of warfare and brutal German occupation had devastated farms, villages, and families in the Soviet Union. Litvin addresses this difficult topic, but he did not personally witness the terrible atrocities or frenzied violence against civilians reported in other sources. There is anecdotal evidence from both civilians and Red Army veterans that the troops in the "follow-on" second-echelon forces were responsible for the worst excesses of violence against civilians. Many of these men had been swept into the Red Army's ranks from prison camps and from the most recently liberated areas of the Soviet Union, which had seen the longest occupation and brutal treatment by the Germans. The military training and discipline of these new conscripts were much lower than that which veteran Red Army soldiers in frontline units possessed.

Did we pillage and maraud? Not openly. It occurred very discreetly at times, but more as an exception than the rule. There was no need to maraud; after all, the honorable soldier needs only an occasional bite to eat and something to drink. And when you are on the attack, there are always captured supplies. We came upon many German supply depots and storehouses during our advance, and our kitchen was always supplied with three times more of everything than was necessary.

Now and then women were assaulted. I recall one incident that occurred beyond the Vistula, in an area where Germans had settled. We were planning to spend the night in a village just down the road.

Our reconnaissance commander decided to send some scouts into the village to ensure it was free of enemy forces. He sent three scouts on the mission—two fellows and Masha, a Cossack woman who served for us as a scout. They headed down the road, and when they reached this village, they found no German soldiers there, only peaceful residents. In one of the homes, our scouts found a middle-aged woman living with two younger women. One of these young women was her daughter. The other was her daughter-in-law, the wife of a son who was now serving as an officer in the German army. Our scouts had a short conversation with them, then turned to head back to headquarters with their report. As they headed out into the corridor of the house, Masha suddenly spoke up: "What sort of indecisive twits are you? Her husband is fighting against you, but you're leaving her alone? Look: She's blood with milk!"[15] The scouts briefly conferred, then raped first the German officer's wife, then the other young woman.

Within a few hours of the reconnaissance troops' return to divisional headquarters, the Polish mother appeared at the headquarters with her two daughters. The Polish woman demanded a meeting with the divisional commander, Dzhandzhgava. He received the woman in his office. Having heard her complaint about the rapes, he ordered all the scouts to form up outside his headquarters, so that the mother could identify the perpetrators. Passing along the row, the Polish woman recognized the two attackers and Masha. Dzhandzhgava ordered them to step out and follow him into his office for questioning. Once inside, the attackers quickly confessed to the crime.

Dzhandzhgava summoned the Polish women and told the mother, "We have found the guilty parties. According to our laws, the guilty must be strictly punished. The punishment is execution." Hearing the word "execution," the Polish woman became agitated. She glanced at her two daughters, and then asked, "But what can be done to keep them from being shot?" Butsol, the political department chief, said, "The fellows can be saved under one condition: if your daughters agree to marry their offenders." The Polish woman's daughter-in-law was already married, so she simply forgave one of her attackers. The other young woman reluctantly agreed to this arrangement, in order to spare the other scout's life. We couldn't find a priest, so the military procurator was asked to preside over the "ceremony," and he quickly pronounced them husband and wife. To complete the cover-up, Dzhandzhgava gave a vehicle to the scouts and permitted them to return to the Polish woman's apartment to celebrate the wedding. The next morning, the scouts moved out with the entire division and marched onward, leaving the young Polish women behind.

Why did Masha behave this way, and urge her comrades to rape? Probably, she had seen how the Germans had treated our own Volga Germans in the Kuban, while it was under fascist occupation. The German occupation of our land was extremely brutal.

To Danzig

The decision to turn Rokossovskii's Second Belorussian Front northwards, toward Danzig and the Baltic coast, was controversial even at the time it was taken. Both Rokossovskii and Zhukov protested against the dispersal of force directed toward Berlin. As the 70th and 65th Armies, along with the 1st Guards "Don" Tank Corps, veered northwards, they left the right flank of Zhukov's First Belorussian Front exposed as it advanced westward toward Berlin. Such ambitious pursuit of divergent goals had led to disastrous consequences for the Red Army in previous years. Only the weakness of the German armies at this point in the war averted a similar disaster. Even so, the decision to split the Second Belorussian Front away from the First Belorussian Front undoubtedly delayed Zhukov's advance. Postwar historians have also criticized the decision. The historian Max Hastings describes the redirection of the Second Belorussian Front away from Zhukov's right flank as "the Stavka's worst strategic decision of the last phase of the war—and the Stavka was, of course, Stalin."[16]

The Second Belorussian Front became enmeshed in the isolation and destruction of the East Prussian group of German forces and the capture of Danzig. While successful, these operations left the First Belorussian Front to contend alone with an unpleasant surprise on its northern flank. On 15 February 1945, the German Eleventh SS Panzer Army under the command of Felix Steiner tried to exploit the First Belorussian Front's exposed right flank in the Stargard area. The Eleventh SS Panzer Army was a motley collection of understrength SS divisions, several of which were of foreign origin, such as the "Wallonian," the "Nederland," and the "Nordland." With a total of 300 tanks and assault guns, the Eleventh SS Panzer Army was still a strong German strike force for its time, but it was clearly too weak even to attain its rather limited objectives. After biting into Zhukov's right flank, the Eleventh SS Panzer Army could not close its jaws around the pocket it sought to create, and the "Sonnenwende" Offensive was abandoned after only three days of heavy fighting. Still, the attack alarmed Stalin sufficiently to slow the advance of Zhukov and Konev on Berlin. The Stavka ordered Konev and Zhukov to hold up the race to Berlin until they had cleared the threat to their flanks in Pomerania and Silesia.

The route to Danzig lay across several river barricades, and in places was covered with forests. We had to take each kilometer, every water boundary, and every populated place from the enemy by combat. The weather was fluctuating, with frequent thaws and sometimes rain—and this was in February. At other times, a wet snow fell.

The alarming situation of the German armies in Prussia had finally forced Hitler to concede to the transfer of some of the divisions trapped in the Courland Pocket to East and West Prussia. The Second Army, which was slowly disintegrating under the constant pressure of Rokossovskii's left-wing armies, received a steady stream of reinforcements from Courland. On the retreat to Graudenz, the Second Army acquired the 83rd Infantry Division, a regiment of which was left in Graudenz to garrison the "fortress." After the left wing of the Second Belorussian Front had crossed the Vistula and turned toward Danzig, the Second Army received further reinforcements from the Courland Pocket, including the 215th Infantry and 32nd Infantry Divisions, and the 4th Panzer Division. Most of the divisions had not had time to recover from the battering they had taken in the fall of 1944.

With the reinforcements from Courland, the Second Army tried to organize lines of defense in the Tuchelder Heide (the Tuchelder Heath), a large forested region west of the Vistula and south of Danzig. The terrain permitted ambush and delaying tactics that took a toll on the attacking armies. But Rokossovskii's divisions preferred to strike at the hastily raised, weakly armed, and inexperienced Volksturm units that were trying to buttress the German lines of defense. Each breakthrough at the points held by Volksturm units threatened the regular divisions with encirclement. Under this constant threat and steady pressure from the Second Belorussian Front, the regular divisions of the Second Army had to fall back to position after position toward Danzig and the Baltic coast.

Somewhere about halfway between the Vistula River and the Cherek River, we stopped for the night and went into camp. The radioman deployed the radio set and handed the earpiece and microphone to the divisional commander. General Frolenkov, Hero of the Soviet Union and commanding officer of the 193rd Rifle Division to our left, was calling. The time was about 5:00 P.M. Our neighbor's right-flank regiment was lagging behind our left-flank regiment, the 1203rd, by about ten kilometers and was in serious circumstances. The enemy moved into this gap and was trying to cut off and destroy the 193rd Rifle Division's lagging regiment. General Frolenkov was asking for help.

The day had been wet, and the roads were in bad shape. The elements of our division had stopped in their march formation. Dzhandzhgava ordered the commander of the 1203rd Rifle Regiment to attack the enemy from the flank and rear with one battalion and a battery of 76-mm guns, to help the neighboring regiment break out of encirclement. General Frolenkov wanted the attack to begin at 9:00 P.M.

Before they started their nighttime attack, Dzhandzhgava wanted all the involved troops to receive a hot meal and get an hour's rest. At 7:30 P.M., I was ordered to bring up my Willys. We drove to the 1203rd Regiment, so that General Dzhandzhgava could check on how preparations were going for the night assault. We traveled just the two of us—no adjutant, no escort, and no radioman. It was dusk when we set out, and dark by the time we arrived at the spot where the attacking battalion was concentrating.

Just before we reached the village where the battalion was supposed to rest, we overtook a column of soldiers—they were wet, filthy, and tired. All four guns of a 76-mm battery were mired in mud to the left of the road near the village entrance. A team of horses was trying futilely to drag one of the guns out of the muck. It was a picture of misery.

We stopped near the guns. It turned out that the column of troops and the mired gun battery were from the designated assault battalion. The general asked the gun teams, "How did you wind up in this mess?" One older soldier, about forty-five years old, answered him: "Comrade General, our battalion commander was just passing through here with some Polish mademoiselle and forced our guns off the road. That's how we got stuck."

While the general talked with the gun crews, I helped give the guns a tow out of the bog back onto the road, which had a gravel surface. When the general asked where the battalion commander was, the older soldier replied that he had driven past about seven minutes ago at the head of the battalion column. By now, it had also become clear that there was no hot food for the men.

General Dzhandzhgava climbed back into the Willys and ordered me to catch up with the battalion commander. This wasn't difficult, as a motorized vehicle moves faster than a horse team. The battalion commander was riding in a sumptuous carriage with an awning. I overtook the carriage, slowly drove around it, and looked inside. The head of this battalion commander was lying on the lap of this dame, and the lady was dressed in bright stockings, a short skirt, and smoking a cigarette. I pulled in front of the carriage and stopped.

As soon as the major spotted General Dzhandzhgava, he leaped down from his seat and rushed to the jeep. "Comrade General. . . . " Dzhandzhgava could tell by his slurred speech and the odor of alcohol that the major was drunk. The general asked him sharply, "Where is your deputy?" Then he ordered the deputy to appear before him immediately. Dzhandzhgava next continued his interrogation of the major, asking him where his battalion was, where the field kitchen was, and what preparations he had made for the attack. The major replied, "There is no kitchen. It's somewhere in the rear. We also don't have enough combat supplies for an attack." At this point, the deputy battalion commander ran up, together with a radioman. The captain said that they were preparing for the attack but had no field kitchen set up to give the men a hot meal.

The general ordered the radioman to let the regimental commander know that the battalion commander had been dismissed from command. We established contact with the 1203rd Rifle Regiment's commander, and General Dzhandzhgava ordered, "Send a kitchen here immediately from any battalion that has a hot meal prepared!" Dzhandzhgava sternly told the intoxicated major to appear before him at divisional headquarters the next morning.

Within about forty minutes, a field kitchen arrived and the troops were fed. But they didn't manage to dry out: it was drizzling rain all the while. After a short rest, they successfully conducted their attack and completed their mission, though truth be told, the attack started an hour behind schedule.

When the major appeared before him the next morning, Dzhandzhgava removed the officer's shoulder straps. Dzhandzhgava ordered, "Three months in the assault battalion!" (We had the 25th Assault Battalion, for officers, in the 354th Rifle Division, and the 261st and 263rd Separate Army Penal Companies subordinate to the divisional commander.) Thus, for knowing when to drink and which road to take while drunk, the major was demoted and sent to the penal assault battalion.

General Dzhandzhgava was a great admirer of discipline. He couldn't stand cowards and punished those who went into battle drunken (that is, he didn't pay any attention to the ordinary soldier in such a condition, but punished the officers).

Regulations demanded unquestioning subordination in the Red Army. But all the commanders and officers under whom I had the occasion to serve and fight behaved properly and treated their subordinates with respect. There were, of course, petty tyrants as well. I never had any immediate contact with one, but I remember a senior lieutenant in a neighboring battery, a Belorussian, who loved to shout: "I've given an order! I have so ordered!" Of course, all officers gave orders, but in my personal experience they always gave them reasonably, courteously, without any arrogance. We carried out such orders more quickly. In general, our commanders were good men, worker-peasants who had risen through the ranks.

Two of our regiments easily advanced within twenty kilometers of Danzig, but the 1199th Rifle Regiment was held up in front of a small hill by firmly entrenched enemy troops. Dzhandzhgava gave the regimental commander Piatenko one more night to take the hill and told him, "Take that knoll at whatever the cost!" That evening, Piatenko gathered together a volunteer force of scouts. They stealthily surrounded the knoll in the darkness, crawled within a short distance of the enemy trenches, and then launched a sudden assault. They quickly overpowered the enemy: of the seventy-two soldiers defending the hill, they took thirty alive as prisoner.

The next morning, when we arrived at the hill, we found no one there except signalers who were winding communication wire. The 1199th Rifle Regiment had taken the hill and moved on. We caught up with the regiment, and as we approached, we saw in the near distance a line of prisoners drawn up in rank. They were Vlasovites who had been captured the night before.[17] Piatenko was walking along the line of prisoners, among which were five or six Uzbeks. I don't know how true this story is, but later I heard from guys who were present that as Piatenko passed down the line of prisoners, he recognized one who had been a classmate of his. When Piatenko slapped his face, another one of the Uzbeks suddenly pulled out a concealed pistol (the prisoners had obviously not been carefully searched) and took a shot at Piatenko. The bullet struck Piatenko but gave him only a flesh wound. We pulled up at this point in my Willys, and General Dzhandzhgava spotted the Uzbeks. He had previously encountered Uzbeks of this sort during the Kursk battle, when several of the Uzbeks among our reconnaissance troops had gone over to the enemy while on scouting missions.

There were two machine guns standing nearby, and General Dzhandzhgava walked over to one of them and fired a long burst at the Vlasovite prisoners, who all fell to the ground. Dzhandzhgava then roared, "Get up, you stinking cowards, you can't even die like men." Dzhandzhgava had fired the burst over the prisoners' heads, since it was formally forbidden to execute prisoners.

That evening, when we returned to Dzhandzhgava's quarters, a military procurator was already there, waiting for Dzhandzhgava. The procurator asked, "Well, Dzhandzhgava, did you execute a bunch of prisoners today?" Dzhandzhgava explained what had happened. The procurator listened in silence, then asked, "And your Piatenko, what did he do?" That night, just in case, Dzhandzhgava summoned Piatenko, wrote out a pass for him, and sent him off to study at an academy in Moscow.

Overcoming resistance of the Germans and their allies, the miserable weather and road conditions, and both small and wide rivers, we reached the Danzig fortified sector, which by that time was occupied by the German's XXVII Corps of the German Second Army—the same opponents we had been fighting ever since our breakout from the Narev River bridgehead.

Rokossovskii was most determined not to get tied up in front of Danzig, as had happened to the Third Belorussian Front at Konigsberg. So he decided to storm Danzig quickly with the 65th Army, the 2nd Shock Army, and other elements of the Second Belorussian Front. The 65th Army attacked through a wooded region to the west of the city toward the suburb of Emaus.

By now, the ranks of our infantry regiments were terribly thin. The command tried to reinforce the frontline units, but even after this, they had only about 40 percent of their regulation numbers. We could no longer count upon numbers for victory but had to rely upon ability and firepower. If instead of 3,000 men per regiment, there now remained only 700 to 800, and battalions had dwindled to the size of companies (120 to 170 men). Our artillery strength, however, was more than sufficient. We now depended upon our artillery; wherever German resistance was strong, we concentrated artillery at that spot. The tanks of the 1st Guards Tank Corps also rendered us enormous assistance in overcoming the enemy's resistance. With their efforts, we managed to break through the fortifications of the outer Danzig defensive belt and reached the outskirts of the city itself.

Here's what one captured staff officer of the German XXVII Corps had to say during his interrogation: "The task of our forces was to offer rigid defense. Your offensive contained many surprises for us. I personally had considered and reported that the 65th Army of Russians was too weak to undertake any serious efforts in the given sector without reinforcements or other strengthening. However, you brought into battle a heavy tank corps, and the situation turned sharply against us."

Danzig

To determine where a suburb ends and where a city begins is practically impossible, and only a map can determine this. The entire coastline of the Danzig harbor of the Baltic Sea, from the mouth of the Vistula River to the Spit of Khel', is a densely populated area without borders or gaps. Thus, three coastal cities, Danzig, Sopot, and Gdynsk, merged into one enormous metropolitan area, stretching along the coast for approximately forty-five kilometers.

Our headquarters stopped in Danzig's suburb of Emaus. An enormous port, a naval base, and an inaccessible fortress of stone and brick with thick walls and underground corridors and bunkers—this was Danzig.[18] The Danzig garrison was supported by the fire of naval artillery from the ships of the German fleet located in the bay. However, the German air force was weak here, and limited in its ability to trouble us.

In contrast, our air force reigned supreme in the skies above Danzig. Here for the first time I managed to see the enormous armadas of our air force. Primarily, they were bombers and close support IL-2 "Shturmoviki" flying in divisions and corps. Up to sixty to eighty fighters provided cover against enemy fighters for each bombing raid.

At times when our radios were not being used for conferences, our radiomen liked to tune into the frequencies of our bombers and listen in on their conversations. The flight group commanders reported where they were leading their groups. The targets for the groups were various—some flew to work over the ships, others to strike the port and wharves, still others to attack the city itself, enemy troop concentrations, and other ground targets.

The fighting for the city was difficult and bitter. The enemy took cover in buildings that had been previously prepared for lengthy defense. The thick stone walls of the buildings did not yield even to heavy-caliber guns, but it was still necessary to drive out the enemy. Instead of typical battalion and company formations, our command created special assault groups, the composition of which consisted of a rifle platoon, two to four self-propelled guns, engineering detachments, and sometimes flamethrower teams. It was necessary to storm each building, apartment by apartment, floor by floor. Often, we had to wheel heavy artillery pieces into position to fire directly upon a building.

Our assault tactics were approximately the following: The *avtomatchiki* would prepare for the assault. The artillery would fire over open sights at the windows on the lowest level, while the *avtomatchiki* would crawl up to a building entrance. When the *avtomatchiki* had reached to within fifteen meters of the building, the artillery would switch their fire to the second floor, while the *avtomatchiki* would break into the building and mop up the first floor. Then the artillery would raise its fire to the third floor, while the infantry would sweep the second floor of enemy remnants.

Our bombers destroyed many buildings in Danzig, primarily those where enemy troops were deployed, military institutions, storage depots, and also industrial enterprises working for the army. The divisional commander always went on foot to the observation post because it was almost impossible to travel by car: all the main roads in the city were blocked by rubble. The Germans were also quick to spot vehicular traffic and would call down artillery fire on it.

I still recall how artillery fire often shattered the walls of buildings before my very eyes. Building collapses were another danger in the city. Twice I was witness to a building collapse, as I traveled around captured sections of the city. One of the collapses was in the city directly next to one of the parliamentary buildings. I had a close call another time. I was driving in a slowly moving column of vehicles, when the front wall of a building, weakened by shelling, suddenly collapsed just five meters in front of me and crushed one of our antiaircraft machine-gun emplacements standing beneath it.

Because of my position as chauffeur, I had little to do during this battle, and I asked permission from the adjutant to take my jeep to the division's auto service company for repairs. But he declined my request then, deciding to delay the repair trip until after the fall of Danzig. Having received this refusal from the adjutant, I tried to fix some of the vehicle's problems on my own, but the steering system in particular defied my best efforts: the steering could fail at any moment.

Approximately 25 March, our command post changed positions and took up residence in the second parliamentary building. Our final assault on the city began 26 March. By dawn on 27 March, we were entering the city center itself. Our 354th Rifle Division advanced down the Weinbergstrasse and the Karthauserstrasse toward the river that split the city.

On the evening of the twenty-seventh, the divisional commander notified me that he wanted to drive to an observation post the next morning, around 9:00 A.M. The Willys had to be ready by then. We would have to make the trip under enemy fire.

The next morning, the full operational team got into my jeep: the commander, the operational chief of staff, the head of divisional intelligence, and both radiomen and sentries. We drove about halfway to our destination safely, but when we entered the enemy zone of fire, shells began exploding to our left. I drove about 200 meters farther under this fire, when suddenly Dzhandzhgava ordered me to make a right turn. I turned the steering wheel energetically to the right. The wheel turned quite easily, but the Willys continued to roll straight ahead, with enemy shells exploding around us. I knew that the steering system was broken, and I could no longer steer the jeep. I stomped on the brakes, and we all jumped out of the jeep and ran to take cover under the arch of a multistory building. The general asked me what was the matter, and I reported to him that his adjutant had not permitted me to take the jeep for repairs. The adjutant was punished for this, but I also didn't feel like a hero myself.

Putting one of the sentries under my command, the general and the other officers left on foot for the observation post, while the sentry and I remained with the Willys. Somehow we managed to get back to the division's auto repair company in the Willys. Along the way, we dropped by the command post and grabbed a few cigars, cigarettes, candy, and other war booty, which might not be available to the guys back in the repair company.

Heading out of the city, we caught sight of a group of soldiers standing around one particular building. It turned out to have a wine cellar. We poured out up to twenty liters of champagne for later use and grabbed some wine bottles. We continued on our way, but the jeep kept stopping on its own every now and then. Once it stopped by a deployed group of Polish soldiers. During the liberation of Danzig, a tank brigade of the Polish army (the Polish 1st Tank Brigade) fought together with us. This brigade carried the title "Heroes of Westerplatte." A certain Colonel Mamotin commanded the brigade. The brigade had many soldiers who could speak Russian well. So cooperation with the brigade was easy, and they fought as our left-hand neighbor during the battles.

We drove out of the city. The asphalt road gave out and turned into an unpaved country road. It became very unpleasant to crawl under the vehicle, in the muck, to tighten up the steering traction, so we decided to proceed without steering. The road was rutted, and as long as we stayed in the ruts, the car wouldn't wander off the road. In order to make turns, we used an oak stake, about two meters long, that we pulled out of a fence. Whenever we needed to turn, I would stop the jeep, and the sentry would climb up on the front hood. He would rest one end of the stake against the inner surface of a front tire, creating a fulcrum with the jeep's frame, and would then with great effort slowly pull back on the upper end of the stake. In this way, he forced the wheel to turn in the direction I wanted to go.

We reached the repair company safely, in the evening, when the guys were already preparing for dinner. Everyone laughed loudly as we drove up, with a "helmsman on the bow" (the sentry on the hood). To general laughter we completed a full circle of honor and stopped the car by the repair station. Over the three days granted by the general for the repairs, we made all the needed repairs to the Willys. Now we could ride calmly for the next three months.

The Destruction of the East Prussian Group

When I returned to Danzig, the fighting for the city had concluded. Our command post had relocated to a spa zone of the city. Prior to that, the division had been fighting in a dock sector. The division had introduced into battle a training company under the command of Captain Vasilii Vasilevich Grechukha. This company was always under direct command of the divisional commander, and he employed it according to the degree of necessity. The company had just recently held back an onslaught of Germans, who had concentrated by the shoreline in the hope of evacuation by sea.

In a coastal forest park within our division's area of responsibility, the enemy had concentrated up to 5,000 military vehicles and civilian vehicles of potential use to the military, in order to evacuate them into the depths of the country. But our energetic attack and subsequent blockade of the East Prussian group of German forces from the rest of Germany prevented it from evacuating this vehicle depot. Among the loot were trucks and cars from a variety of European countries, America, and even ours; tanks and self-propelled guns; buses and trolleys; prime movers; and other similar vehicles. All of these vehicles were hidden from the air beneath the trees. Most of them were in good working condition, but they all lacked fuel. Our air attacks had prevented enemy ships from mooring and carrying away the vehicles. Colonel Mamontin, the commander of the Polish 1st Tank Brigade, visited General Dzhandzhgava with a request to select several of the vehicles useful for his brigade.

Many officers, specialists, and sailors of the German navy had gathered at the military port, along with the crews of submarines that had come to Danzig for repairs. Altogether, it was about 6,000 men. The German command had hoped to evacuate these men on submarines, but our 105th Rifle Corps had cut off this attempt. Everything and everyone in the port was taken as prisoner or seized.

On 30 March 1945, Moscow saluted our conquest of Danzig, Sopot, and Gdynsk. Stalin expressed gratitude to the troops of General Dzhandzhgava for their outstanding combat performance in taking Danzig (now known as Gdansk).

On 3 April, in the afternoon, the general, Alekhin, and I drove down to the shore of the Danzig harbor not far from our command post. It was quiet, and we wanted to mark our arrival and stay in Danzig by bathing in the sea! But the water was so cold that we instantly hopped out of it.

Thus concluded our march from the Pultusk-Serotsk bridgehead on the Narev River to the shores of the Baltic, at the fortress city of Danzig. Thus was the end of the entire East Prussian group of German forces, which had tried to prevent our troops from encircling and crushing the enemy troops in Berlin. In the fighting for Danzig, we had taken more than 10,000 officers and men prisoner. We captured 140 tanks and self-propelled guns, 356 artillery pieces, and other property, food supplies, and equipment.[19]

To Stettin

Once Danzig had fallen, the Stavka gave Rokossovskii's Second Belorussian Front a difficult task. Rokossovskii was ordered to turn his armies 180 degrees and, while maintaining combat readiness, march 350 kilometers to the west, to take over a line along the Oder currently occupied by sections of the First Belorussian Front. This would permit Zhukov to concentrate his forces for the storming of Berlin. Once in position, Rokossovskii was to launch his armies across the Oder River, cut off the defending Third Panzer Army, press it back to the Baltic, and liquidate it. This would secure the right flank of Zhukov's front as it advanced on Berlin.

By 6 April, our division was moving toward Stettin by foot and in all types of vehicles. A column of vehicles would transport a full regiment, towing its guns and mortars, for about 100 kilometers. There the regiment would unload, fall into order, and continue the advance on foot, while the column of vehicles would return for another regiment and ferry it forward.

On 6 April, my service with the division changed: a chauffeur had arrived for the divisional commander. I turned over my Willys to him and was reassigned to the auto repair company. An assistant for the company's technical section, Senior Lieutenant S. I. Gorshkov, ordered me to drive a captured 1939 Opel Kapitan designated for use by the division's chief procurator, from its place in Danzig to a new location. I started up the motor and heard a tapping from the bearings. I had no time for repairs on the spot but was supposed to deliver the vehicle to the auto repair company's new location, 10 to 15 kilometers from the little city of Altdamm. It was more than 300 kilometers to the 473rd Transportation Battalion's new location.

The road from Danzig to Stettin was superb. The width of the traffic lanes was eighteen meters, and the road was paved with concrete slabs. All turns and crossroads were marked with corresponding signposts. I had never seen such a road before in my life. Rumors circulated among our drivers that this road was called "Hitler's Highway," and that it had been built shortly before the war.

The town in which the auto repair company was located was a few kilometers away from Hitler's superhighway. Nearly the town's entire population had fled beyond the Oder River. The town had been untouched by war, and all its buildings and residences were still intact. The inhabitants had apparently abandoned their homes in haste, since many cattle and much personal property had been left behind. Only five or six ancient men and women, and a lot of dogs and cats, remained in the entire town. In one of the homes, a family had left behind an invalid old woman. Our soldiers accidentally found her, concealed beneath a feather bed, and our medics took care of her.

The Opel Kapitan reached its destination without major problems, and I turned it over to a repair platoon. I was then ordered to take possession of a Ford V-8 truck, found among the vehicular booty in Danzig. The machine had traveled all of 42,000 kilometers and then fell into my hands. I put my Ford into park and began to check all its parts, assemblies, and connections. While I was working, a little yellow shorthaired dog came running up to me. I gave it some food, and it stayed with me until the day's end. The next morning, the dog began to circle around me. I started to train it to the noise of engines and the sound of vehicles. To the satisfaction of my comrades, I named the dog "Goebbels." "Goebbels" fought and served with us until 20 October 1945. It left me in the city of Liuboshin, not far from Kharkov, when we were leaving for the "Kongressovka" sugar factory to turn in my truck for the national economy.

I checked and readied the Ford truck for work. I received an assignment to deliver combat supply to the firing positions of rocket launchers, and ammunition to the rifle regiments' artillery and mortar batteries. Almost everywhere, wherever I traveled, I met old acquaintances among the soldiers and officers. Many of them proposed that I remain with them, but I could not permit myself to do this because I was serving in the 473rd Transportation Battalion.

On the eastern bank of the Oder River before the city of Stettin lay the little village of Finkenwald. One of our battalions was occupying this village. While the mortar men unloaded the shells I had brought to them one day, the battalion commander took me to the observation post, which was located in the garret of a three-story building. I had the opportunity to get a look at what the enemy was doing in Stettin, but at this point the Oder was wide and in two channels, so I couldn't see anything in the enemy's camp.

The Second Belorussian Front confronted a difficult task, even with its enormous superiority in force over its opponent. Along most of the river-front occupied by the Second Belorussian Front, the Oder River flows in two branches, the East Oder and the West Oder, each of which had a span of 150 to 240 meters and a depth of 7 to 10 meters. A series of marshy islands, cut by canals, ditches, and ponds, lies between the two arms of the river. In general, the whole ground is swampy and was flooded at the time of the offensive. The numerous dikes that crisscrossed the flooded terrain became the sole conduits for the movement of tanks and artillery, which allowed the German defenders to zero in on advancing armor. The German defenses beyond the West Oder consisted of three bands of fortifications up to 14 kilometers deep. Batov's 65th Army lay in the shadow of the city of Stettin, within range of the defenders' long-range artillery in the city. However, the Third Panzer Army, which was defending Stettin and this stretch of the Oder River north of Berlin, consisted primarily of a motley collection of naval infantry divisions and volksgrenadier divisions. These inexperienced units could not offer prolonged resistance, but the strength of their defensive position would still test the Second Belorussian Front.

Rokossovskii's task was complicated by the absence of information about the enemy. The elements of the First Belorussian Front that had occupied this stretch of the Oder had themselves just reached the river barrier and were waiting for their relief by the Second Belorussian Front. They had no offensive intentions whatsoever at this point, so they did not conduct any active reconnaissance. To make matters even more difficult, the Stavka wanted the offensive to begin quickly, so that it would follow quickly on the heels of Zhukov's assault farther south.

Given the situation, General Batov ordered a specific, limited attack by his divisions to seize the flood-land between the two arms of the river. This attack would possibly reveal the enemy's strength and system of fire, and improve the army's situation before the primary assault across the West Oder. On the night of 16 April, Batov's divisions used the cover of a dark and foggy night to seize the islands lying between the East and West Oder, and even to seize several tiny footholds on the west bank of the West Oder. It is probable that the Germans were laboring under severe ammunition shortages and did not want to reveal all their firing positions to try and stop the Soviet effort. Feverish work began in the swampy land to prepare for the assault across the West Oder.

By 19 April, troops of the division had concentrated on the islands in the middle of the Oder River for the purpose of launching the offensive on Stettin the next morning. Many weapons and piles of combat supply had been brought to these islands and hidden under the trees along the western shores. Starting on the evening of the nineteenth, a strong wind began blowing in from the sea. The wind pushed a high wave into the mouth of the Oder, supplementing the sea tides. The water in the Oder began to rise and to flood the islands, submerging everything on them beneath the waves. Soldiers were forced to raise some supply loads and lash them in the trees, while others made rafts and loaded them with supplies that were not waterproof. They began quickly crafting floats from wooden boards, which they attached to stacks of shells so they could find them under the water. By the middle of the night, the water level had risen by two meters. Some soldiers climbed trees to escape the rising waters, while others huddled miserably on the dikes that crossed the flood-land.[20] The Germans must have sensed when our assault would begin, because around midnight, an artillery cannonade began to thunder from Stettin, and it lasted for two hours. Then it fell silent.

Perhaps nothing demonstrates better the weakness of the German armies at this time than their inability to take advantage of the awkward, precarious position that the rising waters created for Rokossovskii's assault units. However, by this time of the war, ammunition supplies were critically short for most German units, so the defending Germans probably decided to withhold their fire until the actual assaults began.

The Final Assault Begins

Rokossovskii intended to attack the German defenses across a thirty-mile front between Altdamm to Schwedt, using Batov's 65th Army, Popov's 70th Army, and Grishin's 49th Army deployed from north to south. Like Koniev's plans for his First Ukrainian Front's offensive across the Oder, Rokossovskii intended to make ample use of smoke to screen the attacking force. He also planned for large diversionary attacks by the 2nd Shock Army and the 19th Army north of Stettin across the Oder estuary. To begin the offensive, Rokossovskii wanted a ninety-minute artillery barrage to begin at 9:00 A.M.

Batov objected to the proposed start time for the attack because he wanted to make use of the early morning mists. He also wanted to reduce the artillery barrage's duration to forty-five minutes because his staff calculations showed that his assault troops would already be across the West Oder by that time. The rising waters in the flood valley increased Batov's desire for an early start time. In the end, Rokossovskii allowed Batov to begin his offensive at 6:30 A.M., while the 49th and 70th Armies elected to stick with the original plan.[21]

Our attack began at dawn on 20 April, as our assault elements made their way across the West Oder in a fleet of little boats and rafts. Fierce little battles erupted along the western bank, as our leading units tried to gain sufficient space to land tanks and guns. By roughly 8:00 A.M., the waters began receding from the islands. It became possible to cross soldiers, supplies, and artillery to the western bank of the Oder, and our lead units began penetrating the German defense lines.

Approximately 8:00 A.M., the crossing of troops to the western shore began with the help of self-propelled pontoons and ferries. The ferries took into tow up to three to five rafts each, loaded with direct-fire artillery pieces and their ammunition, and brought them to the western bank. Each launch made four or five trips, and by 10:00 A.M., a force sufficient to launch the offensive had been landed on the western shore. At around 10:30 A.M., our large-caliber artillery on the eastern shore of the Oder carried out a fifteen-minute artillery attack on identified enemy positions. For several minutes before the conclusion of the preparatory bombardment, *avtomatchiki* left their cover and advanced behind a rolling barrage toward the enemy's front line. By 11:00 A.M., we had captured the first line of enemy defenses without suffering significant losses. (The casualties were especially light because at midnight the enemy had withdrawn their main units into the rear and left behind only weak covering detachments in the front lines.)

Litvin's narrative now skips several days, probably because he was not directly involved in the assault. I have thus taken the liberty to fill in the gap with information about Rokossovskii's offensive, using primarily John Erickson's masterly study of the Red Army, and Mochalov's history of the 354th Rifle Division.

By evening of the first day of the offensive, Batov had managed to get thirty-one battalions across the river, together with fifty artillery pieces and fifteen SU-76 self-propelled guns. Although the right-hand 2003rd Rifle Regiment had been unable to cross the Oder due to heavy fire from the Stettin fortress artillery, Batov still managed to carve out a bridgehead three miles wide and a mile or so deep by nightfall. This was in sharp contrast with the other assaulting armies, which had decided to follow the original plan of a later start time for the offensive. The 70th Army struggled to create several small footholds across the West Oder, and the 49th Army had been decisively repulsed. This setback was particularly critical to Rokossovskii's plan for the 49th Army to sweep the Third Panzer Army away from Berlin and force it back toward the sea.

On the next day, both 70th Army and particularly the 49th Army continued to make slow progress, while Batov's bridgehead across the Oder began to endure sharp counterattacks of growing size. The limited success of the Second Belorussian Front's attacks south of Batov, and the unconvincing demonstration attacks north of the 65th Army, allowed the Third Panzer Army commander von Manteuffel to concentrate on eliminating Batov's bridgehead.

Showing his flexibility and mastery of maneuver, Rokossovskii decided to reroute his 70th Army and 49th Army through the 65th Army's bridgehead, should they fail once again to establish significant bridgeheads of their own. He also offered Batov the 1st Guards "Don" Tank Corps, as well as reinforcements in bridging equipment. Working furiously, engineers laid down thirty-ton and fifty-ton bridges behind Batov's bridgehead, and sixteen-ton pontoon ferries began operating. Slowly, Batov's bridgehead grew to five miles across and more than two miles deep, and Rokossovskii now had to reroute his entire offensive through the 65th Army's bridgehead.

The Third Panzer Army exhausted itself in unsuccessful counterattacks on Batov's bridgehead, while Rokossovskii managed to pour more and more men and material across the Oder. It was a race that von Manteuffel could not win. Mochalov's history of the 354th Rifle Division notes that the turning point in the fighting occurred on 24–25 April, by which time the Germans had expended all their reserves in fruitless counterattacks while trying to eliminate the bridgehead. On 25 April, the Third Panzer Army began to withdraw. Batov's army headed in pursuit and encircled the garrison remaining in Stettin. At dawn on 26 April, a delegation of the city's citizens approached the lines of the 65th Army's 193rd Rifle Division under a flag of truce, and then the city's mayor appeared. Litvin's narrative resumes at this point.

We seized the city of Stettin before noon on 26 April, without the expected resistance of the enemy. We encountered only occasional snipers and small reconnaissance elements. By order of Stalin, gratitude to the troops of General Dzhandzhgava for crossing the Oder and taking Stettin was announced that evening.

Unfortunately, General Dzhandzhgava's radioman and my good acquaintance, Kostia Shebeko, died in the fighting for Stettin. His death occurred on the western shore of the Oder at the end of the first day of the offensive. The divisional commander had stationed his command post not far from an oxbow lake on the western bank of the river, where it had arrived with the first boats. In the afternoon, when our troops had deepened their breach of the enemy lines up to three kilometers, Dzhandzhgava moved his command post to bring it closer to the front. During the move to the new location, Kostia stepped on an antipersonnel land mine and was critically injured. He died soon thereafter. Many others among the headquarters staff received minor bruises and escaped with just a fright.

After Stettin's fall, the enemy's opposition noticeably weakened, and the tempo of our advance increased.[22] The Germans recognized the uselessness of resistance and began to surrender in large numbers. After 3 May, the flow of prisoners grew into a flood. It reached the point that some groups of prisoners walked into captivity unaccompanied by any of our guards, under the command of their officers, who held passes in their hands from representatives of our forces. After the fall of Stettin, our division took the cities of Stralsund and Barth off the march.

Stralsund appeared peaceful and neat, without a trace of cruel fighting or demolitions. The Germans were trying to save their old cities, and if there was any resistance, it took place not within the city itself but primarily on the approaches to them. On 1 May, Stalin announced gratitude to the troops of Dzhandzhgava for its capture of the city of Stralsund.

The War's End

With the near-total collapse of resistance, the pace of events became a whirlwind. Further such announcements of gratitude from Stalin followed on 3 May 1945 for the capture of Barth, Wittenberg, and the linkup with troops from our English allies, and on 5 May for the capture of the Rügen Islands. With the capture of these islands, the troops of our division fired its final shot of the war, and for us the war had ended. The officers and men of the 354th Rifle Division began unofficially to celebrate the end of the war.

On 8 May, my Ford truck and a ZIS-5 truck with its driver were ordered to report to our division's postal service. There, our trucks were loaded with packages for home, and we carried them to the 65th Army's post office, which was located about thirty kilometers from the city of Yarmen. We turned over our packages there. The day before, my driving partner had been there, where he had met liberated fellow countrymen who had been brought to Germany to work in the factories.

On the afternoon of 9 May, the bustle of communications officers caught our attention. Their soldiers were putting up loudspeakers on the square surrounding the post office. They explained to us that at 5:00 P.M. an important government announcement would be transmitted to the canteen. We had no doubt that this announcement would declare the end of the war. Precisely at 5:00, we learned through the loudspeakers of Germany's formal capitulation. The war was officially over. The other driver and I celebrated the announcement together with the soldiers of the local commandant's office, and with our repatriated countrymen. We conducted our festivities in the home of some rich German, who had abandoned it as the Red Army approached. Only the former servants—three young Russian women and another woman—remained in the house.

We spent forty-eight hours in Yarmen, and on the third day, a column of vehicles under the command of a platoon commander arrived from our division's transport company. We loaded all the trucks, including my Ford, with packages for the men and officers of the 354th Rifle Division, and all set off together back to the division to deliver them.

By the middle of May, the division was moving on a path that took it through Poland once again. We passed Krakow and stopped in the city of Yarotsyn. We lingered there a week, then resumed our march—back to Germany, in the vicinity of Glogau. While driving from Yarotsyn to our new destination, I had the good fortune to visit the grave site and monument to our famous Russian general of the Napoleonic Wars, Field Marshal M. I. Kutuzov, in the city of Bunzlau. I must say here that the Germans had cared for the grave site and tended to it lovingly. Kutuzov had died on this spot in April 1813, as the Russian forces were liberating the enslaved nations of Europe from the French. The body of Kutuzov was later transferred to Petersburg and reburied in the Kazan Cathedral.

The division settled into a military base camp in Shtranse. Here the command began demobilizing our older soldiers and started reorganizing many units and formations. They created the new 462nd Artillery Brigade in our division by combining formerly separate artillery regiments, including the 921st Artillery Regiment, the 633rd Heavy Mortar Regiment, an antiaircraft regiment, and two other regiments. I served with my Ford truck in the 633rd Heavy Mortar Regiment. There was no longer any war, and our trucks with the attached rocket launchers were parked in storage.

Many more soldiers from the division were demobilized in the middle of July, including Mariia Baturova, who was no longer a nurse, but now an official in the city of Shtranse. At the end of August, the 354th Rifle Division transferred thirty-three vehicles of Soviet and foreign manufacture to the Soviet national economy. My final duty was to deliver my Ford V-8 to a sugar factory near Kharkov. On 1 September, a column of 400 army vehicles left on the journey to Kharkov. Along the way, we picked up repatriated citizens who were trying to make the long way home. I picked up one fellow and two girls from Poltava Oblast. I was able to take them straight home and to see the joy of their family and friends upon their safe return.

The column stopped in Liuboshin, near Kharkov. On 20 October 1945, I turned over my truck to the "Kongressovka" sugar factory, received a fifty-day furlough, and headed home to Petropavlovsk. I

142   was able to travel for free, since military requirements demanded the collection of tickets from passengers westbound to Germany— but now I was going in the other direction!

My Arrest and Postwar Life

After my furlough, my military service continued in the Northern-Kazakhstan Military Commissariat. On 15 March 1946, I was arrested for the illegal possession of a pistol, which I had picked up as a war prize in April 1945 in the city of New Brandenburg. I had promised to give this pistol to my good acquaintance, Captain Alexander Kobzar, the intelligence chief of the 1199th Regiment of the 354th Rifle Division. Officers were permitted to keep a sidearm. However, I hadn't had the chance to give it to him before my departure from Germany, so I kept it to give it to him upon my return to my unit once my furlough ended. However, I never returned to my unit, as they left me to serve in the oblast military commission. I hadn't turned in my pistol to the commandant's office upon my arrival on furlough because I really wanted to give it to Alexander myself. My younger brother took this pistol without my knowledge and temporarily loaned it to his friends, who turned out to be robbers.

For illegal possession of a pistol, the military tribunal of the Petropavlovsk garrison sentenced me to four years' imprisonment. I was taken with other prisoners to Magadan in the Soviet Far East, and then to the Ol'chansk mine. Fortunately, I received the right to work without guard escort. I worked as a *markschneider*—a sign marker—in the mine's machine shop for six months, then I was transferred to work in the mine's technical warehouse. So I managed to stay out of the mines until my release on 29 August 1949. Within two and a half months, I was appointed to the duty of mine surveyor with the mine's First Section, and I worked as a mine surveyor until I left Ol'chansk for good in 1953.

More happily, I married a telegraph operator, Mariia Vasil'evna Shevchenko, at the end of 1949. While still at the Ol'chansk mine, we had two daughters. In January 1953, we were released from the mine and free to travel to Krasnodar, where my wife's father and older sister lived in a village on the outskirts of the city. On 21 March 1953, I enrolled in the Pashkovskii Agricultural Technical School, in its Department of Soil Construction, in order to complete my studies and earn my degree. In July 1954, I earned my diploma as a geotechnical engineer.

In June 1960, in connection with my entrance into the correspondence department of Krasnodar's Engineering and Construction Institute, I left my work in the village and moved into Krasnodar with the intention of becoming a construction specialist. From 1960 until August 1983, I worked as a geodesic engineer and supervisor for a construction organization specializing in high-voltage electrical lines. After my retirement from this work in 1983, I went to work in an agricultural college's geotechnical engineering department. I worked there until July 2002. At the same time, I kept busy with veterans' work in the city's schools, giving talks on the war and participating in school ceremonies. Since 2002, I have stayed constantly busy with veterans' affairs, enlightening kiddies about the war. I travel two to three times every year to meetings of my generation, of those that lived through the war, and to battlefields of the war: Kursk, the Ukraine, Belorussia, throughout the motherland of our Heroes of the Soviet Union.

My daughters have blessed me with three granddaughters and one grandson. They have all received middle or higher education and found good jobs. Two granddaughters have given me two great-grandsons—Danil, a sixth-grade student, and Timofei, who will start school in 2006.

Notes

1. I Become an Airborne Soldier

1. A large famine swept the Ukraine in the early 1930s. Drought in 1931 and 1932 undoubtedly played a role, but most scholars point to Stalin's policy of forced collectivization as the main factor in the famine. Peasants in the Ukraine slaughtered their cattle and horses rather than bring them into a kolkhoz, and state agents seized grain and produce to break the resistance of the peasants to collectivization, and to keep major cities like Moscow and Leningrad supplied with food.

2. The Young Pioneers was a state-sponsored youth organization, modeled after Germany's Hitler Youth program, with great emphasis on paramilitary training and political indoctrination. Neckerchiefs were a distinctive part of their uniform.

3. This was a badge for outstanding marksmanship.

4. *Kolkhozniki* is the Russian term for people who lived and worked on the collective farms.

5. This was the second time in 1942 that the Stavka had ordered the reorganization of the airborne corps. In July 1942, all ten of the existing airborne corps (save three brigades) had been reorganized into the 32nd through 41st Guards rifle divisions and sent to Stalingrad. In the autumn of 1942, the Stavka ordered the formation of eight new airborne corps. But as Litvin states, this second formation of airborne corps was converted into ten new guards airborne divisions. They were filled with trained parachutists and retained their airborne designation, but fought as regular infantry. For a full discussion of the Red Army's airborne forces in World War II, see Steven J. Zaloga and Leland S. Ness, *Red Army Handbook: 1939–1945* (Phoenix Mill, UK: Sutton Publishing, 1998), 143–154.

6. Litvin maintains that Finnish snipers were employed along this sector of Army Group North's front.

2. Kursk

1. This division was given its honorific title "Sivash" for its role at Sivash in the Crimea during the Russian Civil War.

2. This information was passed up to Lieutenant General Pukhov, commander of the 13th Army, who immediately notified Marshal Georgi K. Zhukov of the prisoners and their information. Zhukov, deputy commander of the Soviet Army and the Stavka representative for the northern region of the Kursk, ordered an alert. In turn, General Rokossovskii, the commander of the Central Front, decided to begin the planned counterpreparation artillery barrage immediately. By 2:20 A.M. on 5 July, the Central Front's artillery went into action.

3. Interestingly, according to the Soviet General Staff study of the battle, the Germans repeated their attacks from the northeast on "Pervomaisk" State Farm on 7 July, this time in larger force with two battalions of infantry and twelve tanks. This attack succeeded in capturing "Pervomaisk," after heavy, at

times hand-to-hand combat and penetrated into the northern half of Ponyri. See David M. Glantz and Harold S. Orenstein, *The Battle for Kursk 1943: The Soviet General Staff Study* (London: Frank Cass, 1999), 116.

3. Pursuit

1. The German policy of robbing from one army group or army to reinforce another reached its breaking point by September 1943. As the battered remaining divisions of Weiss's Second Army fell back behind the Desna River, army group commander von Kluge was asking Weiss to send divisions south to counter a crisis in Army Group South. Weiss replied that his army was down to an average strength of just 1,000 men per division, and his front along the Desna was already riddled with Red Army bridgeheads. Earl F. Ziemke, *Stalingrad to Berlin: The German Defeat in the East* (Washington, DC: Center of Military History, U.S. Army 1968), 167.

2. An unpublished chapter from a published history of the 4th Guards Airborne Division, passed along to the editor from the history's author through Litvin, explains this strange deployment. Litvin's antitank battalion was advancing in reserve with the 9th Guards Airborne Rifle Regiment, behind its sister regiments, the 12th and 15th. Captain Nishchakov's battery was in the advance of the 9th Guards Airborne's regimental column, while the remaining batteries in the 6th Guards Airborne Antitank Battalion were part of the 4th Guards Airborne divisional commander's reserve. The author explains, "As so often happens in war, the situation suddenly changed. The leading airborne regiments, which were deploying for battle, moved off the route of march to prepare for a strike on Gaivoron from the flanks. Captain Nishchakov's battery, receiving no updated orders whatsoever, continued to advance directly toward Gaivoron."

3. SMERSH is a contraction for the Russian phrase *Smert' shpionam* (Death to spies!). This was a notorious counterintelligence unit established by Stalin in 1943 to weed out and track down spies, "defeatists," deserters, and anti-Soviet elements within the Red Army. It arrested hundreds of thousands of officers and men, many of whom were shot.

4. This is not the city of Gaivoron on the Bug River, liberated by Konev's Second Ukrainian Front on 12 March 1944, but a village of the same name in Chernigov Oblast, lying about twenty-two kilometers southwest of the district center, Bakhmachi.

5. Throughout the narrative, Litvin kept referring to "Ferdinands," the massive German self-propelled gun built in limited numbers prior to the battle of Kursk. It came to seem that the Germans had an unlimited supply of these heavily armed and armored vehicles, yet somehow the relatively small-caliber 45-mm antitank guns of Nikolai Litvin's battery always managed to knock them out or force their retreat. In a later interview, I had Litvin examine several photographs of German self-propelled guns. I was able to learn that during the war, Litvin and his comrades referred to all German self-propelled guns as Ferdinands, in a similar fashion to our own troops' tendency to call all German

large-caliber artillery "88s," or, in the confusion of battle, to see any German tank as a "Tiger." Where possible, I had Litvin identify the type of self-propelled gun he and his battery faced. For the most part, they were self-propelled guns of the lighter "Marder" type.

6. For a full discussion of the Stavka's plans, the Kiev strategic offensive, and the battles along the Dnepr River, see David M. Glantz, *Forgotten Battles of the German-Soviet War (1941–1945)*, vol. 5, *The Summer–Fall Campaign (1 July–31 December 1943), Part Two* (privately printed, 2000).

7. M. A. Goncharov, *Golubaia pekhota* [Sky-blue infantry] (Kishinev: Karta Moldavenska, 1979), 30–31.

8. According to the Soviet Ministry of Defense, Guards Lieutenant Bastrakov actually earned his honor for his heroic actions in seizing the village Gubin on 3 October 1943 and then holding it against seven German counterattacks on 4 October 1943. Bastrakov was later killed in action near Cherkassy in January 1944. See *Geroi sovetskogo soiuza: Kratki biograficheskii slovar'* [Heroes of the Soviet Union: A short biographical reference], vol. 1, *Abaev–Liubichev* (Moscow: Voennoe izdatel'stvo, 1987), 126.

4. I Become a Chauffeur

1. Litvin's subtle description of the German counterattack probably places the date of this episode as 4 October or 5 October 1943. On these dates, the Germans launched a series of heavy counterattacks against the Dnepr bridge-heads in this area, trying to eliminate the threat they posed to Hitler's "East Wall" and to Kiev. Elements of the 7th and 8th Panzer Divisions managed to recapture Chernobyl' and to split the Red Army's bridgehead across the Pripiat' River into two, and drove back the 18th Guards Rifle Corps from the village of Ditiatki several kilometers. However, in intense fighting, the 18th Guards Rifle Corps managed to repel further efforts by the 7th Panzer to advance, and ultimately the German counteroffensive failed to eliminate the bridgehead. See Goncharov, *Golubaia pekhota*, 31; and Glantz, *Forgotten Battles*, 586–600.

5. Operation Bagration

1. At a major planning session for Operation Bagration in Moscow on 20 May 1944, Rokossovskii and Stalin had openly disagreed over the plan of attack for Rokossovskii's First Belorussian Front. Stalin wanted a single thrust toward Bobruisk from the direction of Rogachev. Rokossovskii, probably understanding that this was what the defending Ninth Army was anticipating, wanted an additional axis of attack, from the south through Parichi. Dramatically, twice Stalin sent Rokossovskii out of the room to reconsider his stance, yet each time Rokossovskii returned to affirm his belief that two thrusts would be better than one. Finally, Stalin asked, "Can two blows be better than one?" and accepted Rokossovskii's plan. It was an illuminating incident. Rokossovskii, who had been arrested and tortured during Stalin's 1938 purge of the military, showed the strength of his personal character. Stalin, on the other hand,

demonstrated a willingness to listen to his subordinate generals that served him well after 1942. See John Erickson, *The Road to Berlin: Continuing the History of Stalin's War with Germany* (Boulder, CO: Westview Press, 1983), 202–203.

2. Termed *maskirovka* (masking, deception) in Russian, this set of measures was an important part of the Soviet art of war, and the Stavka practiced it skillfully and effectively to mislead Hitler and the OKH time and again. The Soviet General Staff study of Operation Bagration details the security measures that the attacking *fronts* followed to ensure surprise for the planned offensive. These included extensive trench digging and the simulation of minefield construction, to give the impression of static defense; false movement of tanks, artillery, and infantry during the day, with regrouping at night; construction of false roads and crossings; concentration of artillery in secondary sectors, where they would conduct several barrages, then withdraw, leaving dummy guns in their firing positions; extensive simulation of tanks and self-propelled guns on secondary axes; strict radio silence; and routine flyovers by staff officers to monitor *maskirovka* discipline. See David M. Glantz and Harold S. Orenstein, *Belorussia 1944: The Soviet General Staff Study* (London: Frank Cass, 2001), 43–44, 56–57.

3. Ibid., 62–63.

4. This is an interesting point. If the special assault battalion, as the lead force in the attack, had to march two days to make contact with the German defenses, this suggests that the main attacking forces for the First Belorussian Front were held back a considerable distance from the front lines before the offensive. If so, this was a clear part of the Stavka's deception measures.

5. This was a multiple rocket launcher that, depending upon the version, could launch sixteen rockets of 132-mm caliber or thirty-two rockets of 82-mm caliber. "Katiushas" were mounted on a variety of chassis during the war, including unarmored tractors, light tank chassis, and trucks. Their wailing sound on launch led to the nickname "Katiusha" ("Little Kate") after a popular song of the time. Although they were inaccurate and slow to reload, their heavy firepower salvos could be devastating.

6. These units had been created under Stalin's famous "Not a Step Backward" order in the dark days of the summer of 1942. Their purpose was to prevent cowardice in battle and to compel retreating soldiers to return to the fight. They were authorized to execute fleeing soldiers on the spot, if they did not respond to orders to halt and return to battle.

7. These twin-barreled 20-mm cannons were widely used for antiaircraft defense.

8. The Germans had captured General Andrei Andreivich Vlasov, commander of the 2nd Shock Army, on 11 July 1942, when his army was encircled and destroyed southwest of Leningrad. Presumably embittered by what he considered to be disastrous leadership and contemptuous neglect of the army and people by the Bolshevik regime, he agreed to collaborate with the Wehrmacht and proposed the creation of a Russian Liberation Army (RLA), composed mainly of Soviet POWs.

6. Into Poland with the 354th Rifle Division

1. P. I. Batov, *Ukaz. Soch.*, 413; as cited by V. A. Mochalov, *354-ia v boiakh za rodinu* (Penza: Administratsiya Penzenskoy oblasti, 1996), 144.

2. For most prisoners of war on the Eastern Front, it was not a question of whether or not they would die in captivity, but when and how. Prisoner executions were a matter of routine on the Eastern Front. Even if a prisoner avoided execution, his chances of surviving captivity in slave labor conditions were also small. As Max Hastings observes, "Neither Germans nor Russians readily offered quarter, save when prisoners were required for intelligence purposes, or more slaves were needed for their respective mines and factories. . . . Only a minority of Germans who attempted to surrender reached PoW camps." For a fuller discussion of prisoner executions, see Max Hastings, *Armageddon: The Battle for Germany, 1944–1945* (New York: Knopf, 2005), 109.

3. Most of the detail for the historical commentary accompanying this section of the memoir comes from an English translation by Joseph G. Welsh of Rolf Hinze, *East Front Drama—1944: The Withdrawal Battle of Army Group Center* (Winnipeg, Canada: J. J. Fedorwicz, 1996).

4. This is Hill 181.2 as marked on German maps and as discussed in German histories of this operation. Hill 181.2 was occupied by elements of the 5th SS Panzer Division "Wiking" on 22 July, as the southern thrust to cut off the lead elements of the 65th Army tried to close the ring at Kleshcheli.

5. Litvin does not mention casualties, but they were apparently heavy. A German history of this fighting for Kleshcheli and Avgustinka says that elements of the 354th Division were surrounded by the 5th SS Panzer Division "Wiking" Panzergrenadier Regiment "Germania" near Avgustinka and wiped out. The repeated assaults on the hills north of Czeremcha were also costly to the 65th Army. See Hinze, *East Front Drama*, 276–277.

6. In his memoirs published in 1968, Marshal K. K. Rokossovskii writes that air reconnaissance and signals intelligence suggested the threat of a German attack on the Narev bridgehead, but that Batov brushed off the *front* command's warnings because of the total calm reigning around his bridgehead. Rokossovskii adds that Batov even decided to withdraw certain frontline units prior to the German attack, in order to conduct field training exercises in the rear. Rokossovskii, *Soldatskii dolg* [A soldier's duty] (Moscow: Voennoe izdatel'stvo, 1968), 295.

7. In his memoirs, Rokossovskii writes that only Soviet artillery, firing over open sights from the eastern bank, prevented the Germans from crushing the bridgehead. Ibid., 296.

8. Fortified district units, as their name implies, were originally created to man static, fortified positions on the boundaries of the Soviet Union. They were essentially regiment or brigade sized and consisted of three or more machine-gun–artillery battalions. These battalions were heavily equipped with machine guns, mortars, antitank rifles, and antitank guns, and as they followed the advancing Red Army westward, they were used to occupy positions previously

won by the mobile Red Army formations in order to free them for further advances.

9. In the Soviet Union, Jews were considered a nationality, just like Russians, Estonians, Georgians, and so on.

7. The Final Offensive

1. The date of the Soviet January 1945 offensive was advanced about a week out of political considerations vis-à-vis the initial successes of the German Ardennes offensive. However, Stalin probably understood that the Ardennes offensive had weakened the German position on the Eastern Front, and with his massive quantitative superiority in men, artillery, and armor, the offensive to the Vistula River and beyond would not be harmed by starting a week sooner.

2. Brigadier General Codne, "Employment of the 7th Panzer Division with Emphasis on Its Armored Group," in David M. Glantz, ed., *The 1986 Art of War Symposium: From the Vistula to the Oder: Soviet Offensive Operations—October 1944–March 1945, A Transcript of Proceedings* (Carlisle, PA: Center for Land Warfare, U.S. Army War College, 1986), reprinted with additional maps in 1999 by David M. Glantz as a self-published study.

3. Colonel A. von Garn, "Employment of Infantry Regiment 7 of the 252nd Infantry Division of XXVII Army Corps," in *1986 Art of War Symposium*, 435–450.

4. Ibid.

5. Codne, "Employment of the 7th Panzer Division," in *1986 Art of War Symposium*, 459–466.

6. The "Andriusha" was a later version of the "Katiusha" that launched heavier, 300-mm caliber rockets.

7. In the 65th Army's sector, there were 256 artillery gun tubes per kilometer of front, and artillery pieces were standing literally wheel to wheel. For the first time, according to the history of the 354th Rifle Division, there were no concerns about artillery supplies, and the guns fired practically with no limits. However, a dense fog somewhat limited the effects of this preparatory barrage, as the artillerists had to fire blindly at predesignated map coordinates. Mochalov, *354-ia v boiakh za rodinu, 170.*

8. The 65th Army's main blow fell upon the German 35th Infantry Division and the left and center of the 252nd Infantry Division. The 65th Army attacked primarily with masses of infantry, holding back its armor by plan. By evening of 14 January, the 65th Army had actually reached the third and final line of trenches in the first defensive line, and during the night the remaining organized elements of the 252nd Infantry Division retreated to the second line of defenses. Von Garn, "Employment of Infantry Regiment 7," 445.

9. Mochalov, *354-ia v boiakh za rodinu,* 172.

10. Indeed, German resistance after the initial breakthrough, as noted by Colonel D. Glantz in his thorough "Overview of the East Prussian Operation: January–February 1945" for *The 1986 Art of War Symposium,* "was so scattered and weak that very seldom did full [Soviet] rifle divisions or rifle corps have to deploy for combat. Usually, the forward elements handled the defenses

they faced and overcame them until [the armies] reached the Vistula." Glantz, "Overview of the East Prussian Operation," 332. As a sign of the chaos in the German forces during the retreat from the Oder and Narev rivers, on 24 January the 252nd Infantry Division had only four of its own infantry battalions, while it had picked up four battalions and two or three single companies from other divisions. Von Garn, "Employment of Infantry Regiment 7," 449.

11. This is present-day Gruziadz.

12. Actually, establishing the bridgehead was a difficult task for the 1199th Rifle Regiment. Upon crossing, the men had not yet managed to dig in when they were struck by a sharp counterattack that threw them back across the river. As the divisional history notes, "The divisional commander did not greet this news with enthusiasm." Dzhandzhgava ordered the 1199th's commander, Piatenko, to return to the west bank of the Vistula "at all costs." That evening, the 1199th tried twice to recross the river over the thin ice, and twice they were stopped short of their goal. Only a battalion of the 2003rd Regiment managed to cling to its positions on the west bank of the Vistula. It was not until 29 January that the 354th Rifle Division managed to get a bridge thrown across the river and get most of its infantry and light artillery across into the bridgehead. Mochalov, *354-ia v boiakh za rodinu*, 174–175.

13. According to the situation maps in Glantz's "Overview of the East Prussian Operation," the German units trapped in Torun were the 31st and 73rd Infantry Divisions, and doubtlessly other cut-off, disorganized elements of the retreating German armies. Around 31 January 1944, this cut-off garrison of Torun, numbering approximately 30,000, tried to break out to the northwest, toward the crossing over the Vistula River at Kulm. This breakout advanced in the rear of the Second Belorussian Front's 70th Army and did present a possible danger to the 65th Army's artillery and rear services still positioned on the Vistula's east bank.

14. This brief narrative about Fortress Graudenz was drawn from Russ Schneider, *Gotterdammerung 1945: Germany's Last Stand in the East* (Philomont, VA: Eastern Front/Warfield Books, 1998), 269–276.

15. "She's blood with milk!" This is a casual Russian compliment of the time referring to an attractive, plump young woman, normally of peasant stock.

16. Hastings, *Armageddon*, 275.

17. This was a term given to any former Red Army soldier or Soviet civilian who joined the enemy forces.

18. At this time, Danzig was also packed with hundreds of thousands of German refugees from East Prussia, all trying to escape the wrath of the avenging Red Army.

19. Between 13 January and 25 April 1945, Second Belorussian Front suffered 159,940 casualties in dead and wounded. If we combine those numbers with the 421,763 casualties in the Third Belorussian Front, we can see the high cost of the East Prussian operation to the victorious Red Army. During these three months, the Red Army in East Prussia suffered nearly as many casualties as did the Anglo-American armies in the entire campaign between Normandy and the Elbe. Hastings, *Armageddon*, 292.

Notes

20. One soldier in the 354th Rifle Division described the suffering: "Legs became numb from the icy April water, we could no longer feel our own bodies. . . . For an entire hour, we moved around in the water, until someone on the eastern shore noticed and reported our pitiful situation, and the command of a sapper battalion quickly sent boats to our aid. In the boats it became even colder. We shook uncontrollably and our teeth chattered endlessly. We thought we would never reach the safety of shore, so hard were our hearts pounding and shaking together with our bodies." Mochalov, *354-ia v boiakh za rodinu,* 187.

21. Erickson, *The Road to Berlin,* 574.

22. With the fall of Berlin and Germany's capitulation now certain, some German commanders were determined not to sacrifice more men for a hopeless cause and were equally intent not to let their remaining men fall into the hands of the Red Army. Defying orders to hold a defensive line, his army group commander Heinrici permitted von Manteuffel to withdraw with all due speed westward, into the lines of the British 21st Army Group.

Selected Bibliography

Erickson, John. *The Road to Berlin: Continuing the History of Stalin's War with Germany.* Boulder, CO: Westview Press, 1983.

Geroi sovetskogo soiuza: Kratki biograficheskii slovar' [Heroes of the Soviet Union: A short biographical reference], Vol. 1, *Abaev–Liubichev.* Moscow: Voennoe izdatel'stvo, 1987.

Glantz, David M. *The 1986 Art of War Symposium: From the Vistula to the Oder: Soviet Offensive Operations—October 1944–March 1945, A Transcript of Proceedings.* Carlisle, PA: Center for Land Warfare, U.S. Army War College, 1986.

———. *Forgotten Battles of the German-Soviet War (1941–1945),* Vol. 5, *The Summer–Fall Campaign (1 July–31 December 1943), Part Two.* Privately printed, 2000.

Glantz, David M., and Harold S. Orenstein. *The Battle for Kursk 1943: The Soviet General Staff Study.* London: Frank Cass, 1999.

———. *Belorussia 1944: The Soviet General Staff Study.* London: Frank Cass, 2001.

Goncharov, M. A. *Golubaia pekhota* [Sky-blue infantry]. Kishinev: Karta Moldavenska, 1979.

Hastings, Max. *Armageddon: The Battle for Germany 1944–1945.* New York: Knopf, 2005.

Hinze, Rolf. *East Front Drama—1944: The Withdrawal Battle of Army Group Center.* Winnipeg, Canada: J. J. Fedorowicz, 1996.

Mochalov, V. A. *354-ia v boyakh za rodinu* [354th Division in the battles for the Motherland]. Penza: Administratsiya Penzenskoy oblasti, 1996.

Rokossovskii, K. K. *Soldatskiy dolg* [A soldier's duty]. Moscow: Voennoe izdatel'stvo, 1968.

Schneider, Russ. *Gotterdammerung 1945: Germany's Last Stand in the East.* Philomont, VA: Eastern Front/Warfield Books, 1998.

Zaloga, Steven J., and Leland S. Ness. *Red Army Handbook: 1939–1945.* Phoenix Mill, UK: Sutton, 1998.

Ziemke, Earl F. *Stalingrad to Berlin: The German Defeat in the East.* Washington, DC: Center of Military History, U.S. Army, 1968.

Index

Index